The Transition to the New Age

THE ASTROLOGY OF PERSONALITY (1936): A Reinterpretation of Astrological Concepts and Ideals in Terms of Contemporary Psychology and Philosophy.

THE PULSE OF LIFE (1942): New Dynamics in Astrology.

THE FAITH THAT GIVES MEANING TO VICTORY (1942)

THE RHYTHM OF HUMAN FULFILLMENT (1966): A Cyclocosmic Approach to the Basic Problems of our Time.

AN ASTROLOGICAL STUDY OF PSYCHOLOGICAL COMPLEXES AND EMOTIONAL PROBLEMS (1966)

THE LUNATION CYCLE (1967): A Key to the Understanding of Personality.

OF VIBRANCY AND PEACE (1967): An Anthology of Poems.

THE PRACTICE OF ASTROLOGY (1968): As an Integral Approach to Human Understanding.

TRIPTYCH (1968): Gifts of the Spirit, The Way Through, The Illumined Road.

*

ASTROLOGICAL TIMING

The Transition to the New Age

DANE RUDHYAR

HARPER COLOPHON BOOKS
Harper & Row, Publishers
New York, Evanston, San Francisco, London

For TANA

In the faith that she will unfold
in creative strength and peace
the potentialities of her essential being, through the crucial
decades ahead.

D. R.

Originally published in 1969 by Servire Publications, Wassenaar, the
Netherlands under the title BIRTH PATTERNS FOR A NEW HUMANITY.

ASTROLOGICAL TIMING. Copyright © 1969 by Dane Rudhyar.

First HARPER COLOPHON edition published 1972

LIBRARY OF CONGRESS CATALOG CARD NUMBER: 78-184653

STANDARD BOOK NUMBER: 06-090260-4

CONTENTS

PROLOGUE

WHERE DO WE STAND TODAY?

The Historical and Astrological Approaches

It seems hardly necessary to emphasize the fact, now so evident to all perceptive human minds, that we are living in a period of tremendously accelerated change, a period of unparalleled technological, social, cultural and psychological upheavals and transformations. Yet, while this fact is widely recognized and constantly publicized, only a minority of human beings are not only really aware of its implications, but ready and willing to face these implications, both as individual persons and as members of a national and cultural collectivity. This evidently is not a new situation; for whenever a society has been confronted with some radical changes only a minority of its people have ever been truly aware of what was happening or ready to reorient their minds and patterns of personal and group behavior. But today the situation has implications not only more far-reaching than ever in recorded human history, but also more catastrophic if nothing "unusual" happens to repolarize and redirect the present world-wide trends. These world-wide trends of themselves can only lead to an orgy of violence and dying born of the senseless pride, hunger and despair which today are fast reaching an apocalyptic climax.

In our era of world-wide communication and at least superficial mass-thinking, no human being can be willing and ready to face the prospect of radical reorientation and social reorganization on a global scale unless he or she at least dimly understands what is happening and the process which led to such compelling and apparently irreversible events. The only alternative to understanding is an almost blind faith in the teachings and an equally blind obedience to the dictates of some religious leader around whom an aura of divine power, wisdom and love has been built in some more or less spectacular manner. But even in this case it is clear that today such a leader is more or less compelled to give to his words some sort of intellectual, moral and historical background in order to re-set into new patterns of response the restless and distracted minds of the men he must reach in order to fulfill his mission. He must explain the historical process, interpret the facts of today, present a vision of the future -- however irrational his approach may seem to more sophisticated, college-trained and science-worshipping minds.

How can we really understand what has been happening in the world of human beings since a hundred or two hundred years? Superficially, of course, it is easy to list transforming political events, new concepts, new discoveries, growth of industry and technology at a totally unprecedented rate, the fabulous increase in productivity resulting from the release of ever more tremendous powers and from the consequent redistribution of population and the prolongation of human lives leading to an almost catastrophic increase in population, all over the globe. The question remains in the inquisitive mind refusing to be over-awed by scientific achievements: Why this almost sudden outburst? This question demands some kind of answer, and what is happening to mankind has to be, if not "explained", at least interpreted in terms of a large evolutionary, biological or spiritual, and if possible cosmological or metaphysical picture.

An interpretation is necessary, I claim, even though the strictly existential bias and the "scientific" agnosticism of our day may insist that all that matters is to face the facts as they are now, and to respond to them with the best of our mental capacities, perhaps with the help of some mysterious intuition or creative power which somehow seems inherent in human nature. But "facing the facts now", although it sounds good to many ears, actually of itself means very little. Who is to face the facts -- or rather what in a human being is to do the facing?

A man may want to respond wisely and creatively to a new situation; but what is it that does the responding? There are cases undoubtedly in which an individual confronted by a life-or-death emergency unlike any one he has met before will perform the "right action" -- and he may thank for this either divine Providence, a Guardian Angel, or a Soul-intuition, or some form of biological or psychic instinct of self-preservation. But when have we seen collectivities, even when confronted by a life-or-death situation, do the really right actions at the proper time and with total courage -- rather than "too little and too late"? Did the French aristocracy of the eighteenth century, or the Russian aristocracy of the twentieth century, or post-World War II France facing a new situation with regard to her colonies in Indo-China and Algeria face historical-social facts which were of crucial importance to healthful survival, or survival pure and simple? Are we in the United States today, confronted with the plight of our Negro population inherited from centuries of slavery and (later) of prejudice and neglect, meeting "instinctively" and with success the facts of our national life?

The privileged classes in our modern cities (acting like the aristocracies of the past), or indeed all nations now playing poker-games on the brink of almost incredible nuclear disaster, are apparently unable (and mostly unwilling) to give constructive and radically new creative answers to the totally new problems posed by a couple of centuries of vertiginous changes which are putting everything human into question. Why is it so? Simply because the minds and emotions of human beings are set according to social, cultural and religious-ethical patterns which mold the socio-biological and spiritual environment within which these minds and emotions must develop from infancy up to a more or less conformistic maturity.

I repeat: What is it in a man that can make the right and creative answer to an almost completely new situation when the mind, the feeling-responses and the bio-psychic drives of the man are set according to a tradition dominated by past values and an obsolete approach to change? Here and there strong individuals may question and rebel against these traditional values and patterns of living, thinking and feeling; but if these men are not to be satisfied with wild and senseless acts of revolt born of tragedy, frustration and despair -- or, among the more intellectual class, produced by a feeling of total emptiness and boredom -- they inevitably have to base their conscious and enlightened action on an objective study of the past, a study which can also reveal something of the future.

How can we gain a valid (even if only tentative and incomplete) knowledge of the future? How can we orient ourselves today toward some expectable future, and make a constructive, sensible and as little wasteful as possible transition from this today to tomorrow? This is the great problem confronting at this time all perceptive, responsible and creatively oriented individuals. To this problem two basic solutions can be given.

The first, and today most "official", solution is to extrapolate what we know of the past into the future just ahead of us. A whole science, called in France "prospective", is being built, and its perhaps slightly less formal equivalent is spreading fast as well in our country. A number of organizations and specialized firms are busy with selling to large corporations (and as well to the Government and to city-planning commissions) "profiles" of expectable future trends in this or that area of our national economy. These estimates of potential growth (of production, group-behavior and population) and of probable discoveries or achievements in specific fields (industrial and military, here and as well in other countries) are based on statistics, on curves of previous growth, and on various more or less imponderable factors (for instance, what would the Russian Government do in this or that situation, or how would the general public react to this or that new promotion scheme or new gadget). The analyst establishes the speed at which human productivity and social changes have occurred in the past centuries and millennia, and from these data they calculate what the situation will be ten or fifty years ahead.

This can produce evidently very interesting and valuable results; but it takes for granted that processes already started will unfold at a rate determinable by past performance. There is, however, a major flaw in this entire procedure. What the flaw is can be most simply illustrated by taking the example of the physical growth of a child from birth to, say, age seven. Suppose that some beings from another world who have never seen mature human bodies happen upon a group of children between these ages, steal them and leave our planet. Their scientists might determine the rate of growth of human bodies from birth to seven; but if they were to project this rate into the future they might believe that at the age of 30 human beings are great giants.

This illustration may sound very fanciful, yet it actually applies to modern science's approach to the universe. We speak of "universal laws", and on the basic of our calculations we somewhat pontifically give expert opinions concerning the age of the universe, what has happened and will happen to our solar system and the structure of our planet, the drift of continents, etc. All of this is based upon the concept that "evolution" (cosmic, planetary, biological, mental) progresses more or less in a straight line (even if with relatively small ups and downs in the process).

But how do we know that these "laws", not only apply unchanged to the whole universe, but are the same today as they were at the time when this universe was just "born"? We take for granted this unchangeability of our "universal

constants"; but why should we? Nothing around us suggests
that we should, simply because all that we see and experience has a beginning and an end, and the process of unfoldment from beginning to end proceeds according to varying
rates of growth and decay. Why should we believe, for instance, that the force that we call gravitation has always the
same strength?* Is the "vitality" of a living organism the
same in its infancy as when it approaches organic disintegration?

Our official mentality retains still the basic character of
nineteenth century thinking. New scientific cosmologies are
challenging these old concepts, but only hesitatingly and without really accepting the possibility that our universal constants might be dominated by the rhythm of an immense cosmic process which introduces "cyclic" patterns of change.
We still believe most of the time in a straightforward ascent of humanity from primitive "barbarism" to ever more
glorious "civilization".

This concept is a typically "Western" concept. In contrast to it we have the more characteristically "Oriental"
picture of a "cyclic" universe or even more of a multiplicity
of universes, each of which is a cosmic Whole which is born,
develops, matures and disintegrates after a moment of perfect fulfillment -- a fulfillment which nevertheless leaves
"ashes" -- that is, waste material, drop-outs and "karmic"
residua -- to be reincorporated into another universal Whole,
a Whole different from the first, but not essentially "super-

---

*That this idea that I have often stated for many years is
no longer too startling for the modern scientist is shown by
the great physicist Fred Hoyle's new book "Galaxies, Nuclei
and Quasars" (Harper and Row) in which he says that gravitational attraction between bodies may not be a universal
constant and the behavior of matter may vary with different
planets or solar systems.

ior". Each universe represents the working out of an immense set of potentialities; but as potentialities of existence
and of cosmic Wholes of existence are infinite, there is no
end and no beginning to the process of existence. The concept of progress -- in the usual, ethically colored sense of
the word -- can be applied to the vast cosmic and planetary
movement which leads to the perfect actualization of the initial birth-potential of the cosmic or planetary Whole; but,
symmetrical to it, there is also a process of "devolution" or
disintegration, that is, a constant dropping out of unusable
waste materials and of what one might call (relatively speaking) evolutionary failures.

The basic fact is that the entire process is cyclic. Unfortunately since the Council of Constantinople in the fifth
century, Western thinkers are conditioned by their culture
to think of cycles in terms of exactly repetitive sequences of
events; and Nietzsche, (to satisfy his own psychological
need) glorified and popularized this type of thought in his
poetic picture of an "Eternal Return". I believe, however,
that a reformulation of the concept of cyclic process
is today of crucial importance; for without a clear and sound
understanding of what the concept of "cycle" implies -- and
especially does not imply -- our present attempts at or-
ienting ourselves toward the future of humanity in terms of
"prospective" will lead us to conclusions, and make us depend upon procedures, which are likely to prove both useless and destructive.

STRUCTURE VS. CONTENTS

The concept of cycles makes little sense, in terms of any
broad cosmological picture of existence, unless we differen-
tiate clearly between structure and contents. This concept
refers to the structure of the vast flow of existence, but
not to the contents of this flow. Existence is a process of unceasing changes. But man has realized for many
millennia that the forever changing events which affect his

senses and the organic rhythms of his body and psyche display certain definable patterns of recurrence which make the events yet to come to some extent predictable. What is predictable, however, is not the total existential situation including all perceptible or conceivable events in the world, but only certain configurations or gestalts relative to special sets of events isolated by the mind from the total picture of existence.

This is a very important statement which obviously cannot be verified in any absolute sense, but which is at the very root of man's experience of existence. When we speak of cyclic processes in nature, we are isolating definite sets of events the pattern of which recur. For instance, we speak of a lunation cycle because every so many days we observe a recurrence of the new moon and full moon in a particular relationship to the horizon -- i.e. a full moon always rises in the east when the sun sets in the west. But while there are recurrences of full moons, these full moons change their position with reference to the stars. Moreover as each full moon recurs it throws its lights on events and situations on the earth's surface which are never the same. Likewise we can expect and safely predict the return of spring, but no two springs occur under exactly the same weather conditions and bring into identical living organisms the same chemicals.

In other words, events never repeat themselves exactly; and history never repeats exactly the same events. The beginnings and ends of every solar year, of every century, of the great cycle of precession of equinoxes (approximately every 26,000 years) occur in always different regions of the galaxy, which itself has brought its billions of solar systems and stars to ever-new regions of cosmic space. What this means is that you can never speak of two identical events in the existential sense of the term, event, simply because the infinitely complex network of relationships between all "existents" -- whether they be solar systems, human persons, molecules or atomic particles -- can never be precisely the same; UNLESS we choose to believe that the potentialities of existence and existential relations are finite. Such a belief, however, seems to run against every ingrained human expectation and practically against all that religions and philosophies have ever conceived. Whatever the term, God, may refer to, the fact is that whatever and whenever this term and its equivalent have been used by human consciousnesses, it has always been associated with the feeling and/or the concept of infinity. A Nietzschean type of totally repetitive "Eternal Return" would indeed be the negation of the God-idea. It would also be the total negation of meaning in human existence and of any possible freedom of choice for man.

What repeats itself is not the event, but the p a t t e r n of relatively closed series of events with reference to a particular field of existence. In other words, the flow of ever-changing events is an ordered and structured process. As an illustration let us consider a river. This river, seen in its totality from mountain spring to sea, has a characteristic structure which we can see on a map, and we give it a name; but the water itself, whose unceasing flow is normally contained within the structuring boundaries which the particular features of the land make for it, is never the same. The often quoted Zen saying that you can never bathe twice in the same river is untrue or at least confusing in its imprecision, as so many so-called mystical statements are. You can bathe in the same river, but not in the same water. The distinction is most important and far reaching in its implications.

I can bow reverently before the sunrise everyday; but while it is correct to speak of the occurrence as "sunrise" -- i. e. as a formal configuration relating the sun, the earth, and the horizon of my place of residence -- everything at the existential level that participates in this sunrise scene differs each day in some degree. It is not a c t u a l l y the same sun, nor the same horizon, nor the same human organism -- though the mind within this organism may insist that the "I" is a permanent entity. What is permanent is a certain structure of living processes, a gestalt. The name is the same, but the existential reality of every sunrise scene differs in many ways.

This factor of "structure" when generalized and abstractized, is actually what we mean by time -- that which can be measured by clocks which in turn work according to the motions of the earth (its axial revolution creating the "day", and its revolution around the sun creating the "year"). There can be no process without time; there can be no thinking or feeling (as we normally use these terms) without a time-sequence of events in our body. Whether the time-sequence seems to our consciousness fast or slow has nothing to do with the reality of time, in spite of the fashionable arguments to the contrary -- arguments based on an inaccurate or needlessly paradoxical use of words. And if the present scientific concept of the relativity of time with reference to the speed of an observer has any meaning at all, beside its convenient use in formal algebraic reasoning, this would involve a metaphysical concept of the universe which so far does not seem even to have been formulated.

As all processes of existence imply a time factor, time has essentially a cyclic nature. Time, in its most basic sense, is a structuring factor. For instance, the motion of the earth both establishes the reality of time for our consciousness and primarily structures our organic and psychic growth. The length of an organism's life-span conditions fundamentally its character and the possible scope of its responses to its environment and its awareness. As the life-span increases for man there is little doubt that extremely important changes in human society and human psychology will occur -- indeed, are occurring.

Of course from the strictly existential point of view of the official modern mentality, what appears as the important factors in the change are a vast number of new "events" and new types of interpersonal, social-cultural, economic and political relationships. The historian trained in our present day universities is almost exclusively focusing his attention on these existential, factual events -- and on every bit of information that can be gathered concerning such events. Thus this type of historian sees only ever-changing and almost unpredictable happenings. He does not dare -- and perhaps could not afford to, if he wanted to keep his college job -- to present to the academic fraternity vast structural concepts such as have been thought out by "generalists" like Spengler and Toynbee, to speak only of recent historians. Yet, without such encompassing and "cyclic" historical concepts, what meaning is to be given to the chaotic facts and the confusing events of our century?

Academic historians usually retrench themselves behind the hackneyed statement that history actually does not repeat itself. Of course it does not, if we are speaking of precise events -- though even at that level of existential happenings many very striking parallels and analogies can be pointed out. But if we think of the structure of a cycle of civilization, of definite turning points, crises of growth, collective decisions and characteristic failures of nerves or class-blindness, etc. -- and even of the type of personages who focus as it were the meaning and direction of crises and decisions -- then we can indeed see emerging before our mind's vision the over-all time-pattern which beats, as it were, the basic rhythm of historical changes.

We can visualize such time-structures as well in the field of planetary evolution; and the periodical motions of the planets are the percussion players. The whole universe is indeed filled with rhythm. It is an ordered universe, and this order, in time, manifests as rhythm. The universe is a symphonic structure of infinite complexity; yet within man's field of experience a multitude of rhythms can be recognized, each of which establishes cyclic processes. Some of these processes affect the whole biosphere; others condition the growth and disappearance of human societies and civilizations; lesser ones form the warp and woof upon which the life-patterns of individual lives are embroidered.

It is by studying such structural factors that we can gain the kind of perspective upon the present trends of our society which permits us to foresee the structural outlines of history-in-the-making. What such a study can reveal is NOT precise existential happenings, but rather the rhythm of observable processes. Knowing what these processes have produced up to now, and knowing their structural character and basic rhythm, we can gain a "structural knowledge" enabling us to time rather accurately expectable crises and turning points, and to understand what is at stake in these crises -- thus the meaning of whatever concrete events will take place at these nodal points of a history yet in the making.

Knowing this meaning can be of tremendous psychological value, especially to individuals caught like seemingly helpless corks in the momentum of bewildering whirlpools of events. As Victor Frankl, the great Viennese psychologist, has stated in his books (cf. "From Prison Camp to Existentialism"), a man can stand almost any terrible situation, including torture, if he can see in it some kind of meaning and extract from it the feeling that it is structurally related to some larger pattern of growth, perhaps as a "test"; but men will break down and collapse if even much less strenuous events can only be seen as totally meaningless. The search for meaning is the most vital function of the mind and the feeling-intuition of man.

Most men of course accept unquestioningly the set of values and meanings with which they have been provided since birth by family, religion and culture. But when this set of meanings falls apart and loses its convincing and will-mobilizing power, then psychological chaos is impending. The individual will seek escape in neurosis, psychosis or hallucigenic drugs -- or else, finding in his own individual depth (and perhaps in the very acuity of his tragedy, despair and emptiness) a driving power that as yet had been latent, he starts on his own upon a crucial and often crucifying search for meaning.

Then, however, he may become an easy prey for charl-atans, pseudo-teachers and fortune-tellers; for he must at all cost try to establish within himself a new sense of direc-tion. He must strive to get a clue as to what some to him very mysterious, yet psychologically needed, Power e x-p e c t s of him. He hungers for a knowledge of the future -- whether it be his own personal future, or the future of his people and even of humanity as a whole -- for in this future lies perhaps the revelation of a life-purpose for him, of his place, function and meaning in the universe.

Statistical knowledge and the extrapolation of the past in-to the future offer very little that makes sense to the indivi-dual. Will such a "scientific" approach make much sense to mankind as a whole, if perchance some vast planetary cata-clysm, or the coming of far-advanced "space people", were to render totally useless and meaningless all the curves of predictable growth for the establishment of which millions of dollars are being spent? The basic question today is indeed whether or not the social, psychological and biological or telluric processes and modes of human response which we have known in our limited experience of the past may not be made obsolete and superseded by basically new developments. We can perhaps expect a totally new "mutation" of mankind or a basic transformation of society. Without such a most radical development is there indeed any hope for a humanity faced with massive hunger and nuclear disaster? Any type of extrapolation from the past along lines pursued by official computer-based calculations of probability lose all validity if we are at the threshold of radically transforming events which result from the operation of cosmic or planetary for-ces, or of transcendent superhuman minds. And our academic, political or business mentalities have no way of relating to even the possibility of this kind of operation or "intervention".

There is nevertheless a way of discovering the manner in which planetary and cosmic processes reach points of crisis and as a result may play havoc with all our modern scientific prospects for the future. It is a way as old as thinking man; but unfortunately today a way so filled with distorting accretions and so compromised by psychological vagaries and abuses that it seems unacceptable to minds trained in the logical and analytical techniques of rigorous thinking. It is the way of astrology.

Let us try to see what is actually the essential nature of astrology, and how a combination of basic astrological and historical thinking can be used as a truly meaningful, broad and inclusive method for a deeper understanding of the vast process of change in the midst of which mankind is presently floundering in a state of utter confusion and dismay.

ASTROLOGY AND HISTORY

Astrology is essentially the study of the structuring power of cyclic time over existential events. It is the study of those cycles for the measuring of which the periodical motions of celestial bodies offer us a complex but effectual type of "clock". Astrology is a method based on the assumption, generalized from the most obvious facts of human experience, that every existential process has a beginning and an end, and passes in-between these two events through a series of recognizable and measurable phases or critical points of transformation.

If all cosmic, planetary, biological and psychological processes are inherently "cyclic" as they unfold in time, they can theoretically be approached as "wholes" having a definite and measurable structure of growth. If we can isolate these wholes and study their internal specific time-structure, we can gain a knowledge of their schedule of development; and if we are looking at a particular phase of this development occurring today we can surmise what the coming phases will be in terms of the structural character of the whole we are observing. We can at least time approximately the next turning point and the rate of the process. We do this, however, not in terms of particular events, but in terms of the structure of the whole processes. We are considering the entire cycle; ours is a "holistic" approach.

Let us take an example: If a biologist studies a ten year old girl and tries to tell what she will be in five years, he knows that she will have then passed through the crisis of puberty -- a very basic bio-psychological crisis of growth. He knows this, because he knows how the structural pattern of the life-process of a human female operates. He has before his mind the whole structural development of a woman from birth to death; his approach is holistic.

By contrast, if a modern type of facts-cataloguing historian from some other planet who is entirely un-acquainted with the structural development of a woman's organism were to try to picture what the girl will be at age 15 merely from studying the sequence of events in her life from age seven to ten, he would have no reliable way of making such a picture. The "historical" events of the girl's life from seven to ten may be plotted on a curve, but extrapolating the characteristics of this curve into the future at age 15 would be a rather useless operation; it would not be able to foresee the effect of puberty on the girl's total person. It could not predict puberty; because puberty as such is not to be adequately foreseeable by an intellect which has no understanding of the whole life of a human being from birth to death. Puberty is a structural change inherent in the entire process of existence which we call a human being. Around it an immense variety of events can take place -- some happy, others quite destructive. Back of these events -- the tapestry of life -- stands the structural change which gives direction and purpose to these events and from which a meaning can be abstracted.

If we look at a human life as a series of physical and psychological happenings flowing into each other, all we can actually observe is a continuous series of changes, of challenges and responses, of relationships formed then vanishing, of pleasures and sufferings. We take the position taken by a modern novelist describing in great details a day or year in the life of a person, but never really relating this limited sequence of events to the person as a complete whole having a beginning and an end, a fundamental "individuality" and a purpose (however broad and unconscious or superconscious this purpose may be) -- that is, in the philosophical sense of the term, a "destiny". But can we really understand any organized system of functional activities if we do not study it as a whole, not only in space -- for instance, a body which we see and touch -- but also in time, that is, in terms of the whole cycle of its existence?

I can make in early spring a motion picture of one week in the life of an apple tree; but can the exact description of what is taking place in the tree -- the flower, the appearance of small buds -- help me to understand the meaning and function of that apple tree in a garden? Can the movie tell me about the fruit and the seed -- the apple which, at least in a human sense, is the purpose and "destiny" of that tree? I can describe a day in the life of Richard Wagner, as he is fleeing from Germany in 1848 because involved in the revolutionary movement. Can this description make me understand Wagner's genius, his Tetralogy and the meaning of Bayreuth in the culture of Western Europe?

Likewise can we truly understand the many historically recorded events which occurred in Europe during the eighteenth century if we do not consider them as one particular phase of the development of an identifiable whole which we call Europe, or our present European civilization. This civilization, as Arnold Toynbee should have made it clear for any perceptive and "holistic" mind, is a definable, and as well a structured process. You can see it emerging from the disintegration of a preceding Mediterranean civilization. It has grown through specific phases of growth, according to a sequence which parallels the sequence identifiable in other civilizations. But the parallelism is s t r u c t u r a l, not e x i s t e n t i a l; it does not refer to the exact repetition of events.

If we limit the area to which the field of history belongs to the mere collecting of data and the analysis of documents, then the claim that human Societies (or civilizations) constitute wholes with an identifiable over-all pattern of growth, maturation and disintegration is outside of this field of historical research. But if one defines "history" in such a manner, one has to find a new term to characterize a new discipline of thought which deals with the evolution of mankind-as-a-whole -- and with the growth and decay of the various units of social-cultural organizations, the most recent of which Toynbee defined as "civilizations".

It is only quite recently that we have the possibility of studying the past development of mankind in a global manner -- that is, as it occurred century after century at the same time all over the globe. Spengler's point of view was fragmentary because he was definitely biased; and even Toynbee developed biases of his own, especially in discussing future prospects for our Western Civilization. A very few years ago the directors of the remarkable movement PLANETE in Paris, France, began the publication of a series of volumes "Les Metamorphoses de l'Humanite" in which, century after century, the social-cultural development of mankind is being studied in its general cultural manifestations as it took form simultaneously in all continents. Incomplete as this attempt is (it emphasizes especially cultural and artistic manifestations), it is nevertheless, as far as I know, the first well organized and thorough presentation of a truly global study of Man in society, Man the maker, Man the dreamer of "great dreams". It reveals a remarkable synchronicity in the social-cultural trends manifesting all over the world; and light is thrown upon until very recently little known regions of the globe, especially Africa, which has had also most significant cultures.

As long as Western historians were largely blind to anything that had not occurred around the Mediterranean Sea, there could be no global history, and a holistic and structural approach to the evolution of humanity was even more impossible because such an approach actually requires a "planetary" viewpoint. By this I mean that such a holistic approach must realize first of all the structural wholeness of the planet, Earth. It must be aware of the interdependence of all the various "spheres" which constitute functional areas in the total system of activities of our planet: lithosphere, biosphere, atmosphere, stratosphere, ionosphere, etc. -- and we should add "noosphere", the field of all modes of activity referring to the very extensive and ill-defined terms "consciousness" and "mind".

We still speak rather loosely of mineral, vegetable, animal and human kingdoms; but the term, mineral, is not adequate to tell us about the inter-relationship between mankind and oceanic and atmospheric currents and storms, between the development of civilizations and changes in climates and (beyond these actually perceptible changes) even more far-reaching alterations of the earth's magnetism and of the ionosphere in response to solar winds and most likely to forces which have their origin in galactic spaces.*

It is very well for historians to study old documents and archaeologists or ethnologists to scrutinize the records of

---

*cf. the "Piccardi effect" related to not yet well understood cyclic changes in the behavior of water and various chemicals, an effect which apparently varies with the periodical changes in the angular relationship of the equatorial and galactic planes.

past or still living primitive tribal societies. But such an analytical approach, valuable indeed as it is, can hardly answer significantly the crucial problem which is haunting modern man in a period of potentially catastrophic crisis: where is humanity going? Where do we stand? What can we expect? Something else is needed -- a structural and planetary-cosmic approach which would enable us to integrate our tumultuous present in the vast process of evolution of mankind and of the planet, which is the one home of an essentially global humanity.

The great success of the works of Teilhard de Chardin rests on the fact that he has attempted significantly to give us a global picture of Man's evolution -- with reference to a vaster world-picture. The validity of this world-picture is, however, limited by the fact that it is founded upon a religious doctrine which may not be acceptable to many people of the world, at least in the way it is formulated by the French priest-scientist. In other words, it is essentially a metaphysical picture which is being related, in a masterful yet purposive manner, to scientific theories which also may be at best approximately true, and which new "facts" may alter considerably -- if for instance, the existence of high level civilizations of a million years ago (Atlantis?) were proven beyond doubt.

Astrology in its true nature is not based on a tendencious metaphysics or religious belief. It is founded on facts of common human experience, which it generalizes and interprets. The atomic theory is also based on the generalization and interpretations of facts. The nature of these facts is so complex that they can be observed only by scientists whose minds are conditioned by a rigid training which is not without bias in favor of undemonstrable postulates (as for instance the existence of universal constants). Astrology also has its undemonstrable postulates; but like scientific theories, it can prove its value to the extent that it can make order emerge out of chaos. The "theoretical" physicist of today performs the same function, but his field of operation is different. The chaos with which the true astrologer deals is the chaos of human events -- the chaos of historical data and that of personal life-experiences. To these two kinds of chaos he brings measuring clocks which can reveal the hidden structural order inherent in the serial flow of seemingly unrelated, unstructured, unintegratable, and therefore meaningless happenings.

What algebra is to the immense mass of the experimental data of physics or astronomy, astrology can be to the profusion of historical data collected by historians and archaeologists. It can help us to orient ourselves to the future while giving a new meaning to the present trends.

THE EARTH FOUNDATION

The question which the modern type of intellectual may ask here is the often-repeated one: What have the cycles of the planets and the stars to do with events on this earth?

This question is improperly stated. I repeat that true astrology does not deal with events as such but with the time-structure of cyclic processes on the earth, with points or moments of special emphasis. If astrologers are able to predict certain actual events, historical or personal, it is because human nature today being known for what it is, the astrologer can guess or intuitively sense what the normal response of a collectivity or a person will be when structural changes of a certain type occur, i.e. when a new characteristic phase of destiny begins. Also in many cases what is operating in a successful prediction based on astrological factors is a "psychic" gift and the ability of the forecaster's mind or intuition to "resonate" to certain aspects of the vast Mind of humanity -- which we may call the collective unconscious, or the Mind of God, or whatever we wish.

Structural, or super-sensible and super-rational knowledge, is possible to a human being b e c a u s e he is part of Humanity, which in turn is an essential component in the total field of interdependent activities which we call the planet, Earth. This Earth -- which may well include "kingdoms" of which we have little or no knowledge -- has a definitely structured cycle of evolution; and it is an integral part of the solar system, which in turn is an integral part of the galaxy. The galaxy, the solar system, the earth, humanity are integral and structurally evolving "wholes of activity"; and so is an individual human being. All these wholes are interrelated as wholes. Currents of energy flow through them, and while it maybe inaccurate semantically to speak of them as "organisms" they are undoubtedly "organized and integral systems", each of which is in some sense an independent entity, but also all of which are interdependent.

This kind of cosmological picture is the necessary foundation for any astrological thinking that makes sense; and it is a picture which does not differ essentially from what modern science presents to us, though it involves a broader process of generalization of the actually observed facts. Since the Geophysical Year of recent date the fact that every activity within the planetary field of the Earth is closely related to every other activity can no longer be denied. Recently a scientist, Scott Sleeper in San Diego, has pointed to a definite connection between the rhythm of the ionosphere and the alpha waves which represent the basic rhythm of the human brain; and the condition of the ionosphere is demonstrably affected by solar winds and apparently by the grouping of the larger planets within the "field" which the solar system constitutes. This may not lead to the demonstration of the validity of astrology as it is used today, but it should make us realize better that every whole in the universe is related to every other whole, and that every "little whole" participates in some manner in, and is affected by, the structured activities of the "larger whole" in which it is contained.

It seems time indeed for us to realize that man is not something alien and transcendent dropped upon this planet, but that he plays a definite function within the total being of the earth, just as the vegetable and animal kingdoms -- and also stratospheric and oceanic currents -- do. We should give up our proud sense of occupying a special position in the universe as favorites of a personal God, and integrate ourselves -- collectively as humanity, and individually as persons -- in the universe, and first of all in the evolution of the earth. We may reach beyond our planet, beyond the solar system perhaps; but, if we do, this does not mean that humanity will have transcended its structure of destiny. It simply means that, at a certain stage of evolution, man can gain the power to leave his natal home, the earth, and to participate in a vaster, more cosmic field of activity which is also structured by time.

At present, mankind is still enclosed within the planetary matrix in which it has been able, through a multitude of experiences and a knowledge transmitted from generation to generation, to develop a collective mind. What we call "history" is the series of events which have served to develop, culture after culture on all continents, this one Mind of humanity. To know these events is extremely important, but it is not enough, especially today. We should try to ascertain the place and function of this crucial moment of human history -- and as well of our planets' evolution -- within the cycles which structure this evolution; and this requires a type of knowledge which differs from, yet which complements and indeed in some respect depends upon historical knowledge. Structural knowledge -- a knowledge of the complex interweaving of small and large cycles of our planet's evolution -- no doubt extends beyond the concept of our present-day astrology; but the astrological approach at least gives us a significant, even if somewhat rudimentary and uncertain, idea of its fully developed nature.

ASTROLOGICAL CYCLES

Astrology presents us with cycles clocked by the motion

of the earth and the other planets of the solar system. The earth's daily revolution around its axis, and its annual orbital revolution around the sun are basic, yet too rapid to help us to structure the speed of the historical transformation of societies, cultures, nations, and also of slow changes in continents and climates. Other cycles are marked by the periods of revolution of the large planets around the sun, and by the "cycles of relationships" of these planets -- that is, by the periods of years marked by their successive conjunctions. For instance, Jupiter and Saturn are conjunct every 20 years, and every three conjunctions meet in the same zodiacal sign; and this cycle, which was the basis of Chaldean and Hindu "mundane" astrology, has revealed its strange accuracy in the fact that, since the two planets met last century in "earth signs", all U.S. Presidents elected around the time of these 20-year apart Jupiter-Saturn conjunctions have died in office -- and only they.

Another most significant cycle is that established by successive conjunctions of Neptune and Pluto, some 492 years apart on an average; and the last of these conjunctions occurred in 1891-92 marking the initial phase of our Electronic Revolution (discovery of X-rays and radium, Quantum Theory, etc.). Among lesser cycles I might mention here also eclipse cycles (featured in Chaldean astrology), cycles clocked by the motions of Uranus and this planet's conjunctions with Saturn and Neptune, the 13-year cycle of the conjunctions of Jupiter and Neptune, etc. I shall discuss the most important of these cycles in the following chapters.

Then there is another type of cycle which has been greatly popularized of late and which is responsible for the widespread expectation of the so-called "Aquarian Age". This is the nearly 26,000 year long cycle of precession of the equinoxes, and I shall devote the major part of this book to it, for it poses some definite and very significant problems, yet it is the one which has caught the imagination of people sympathetic to astrology all over the world. There are also larger cycles which deal with changes in the orbit of the earth and other factors, but in the present state of our knowledge they are of no practical use. This applies even more to the revolution of the whole solar system around the Galaxy which apparently takes over 200 million years to be completed.

What I shall try to show is the manner in which the cycles which are now of significant value to mankind enable us to bring a sense of ordered structural development to the series of events recorded by history, and how the knowledge of these cycles can situate our present historical situation -- helping us therefore both to understand in a deeper, somewhat "archetypal" sense the meaning and importance of the great turning points of mankind's past, and to orient ourselves toward more or less imminent and inevitable changes. As, I repeat, it has always been extremely difficult for most people (especially for privileged classes or groups in society) to accept the inevitability of such periodical upheavals, the knowledge that they are indeed structurally inevitable (as much as puberty is inevitable in the child's process of growth) and that the time is at hand may help many confused and frightened persons to willingly accept the revolutionary changes.

If such a knowing acceptance based on a conscious realization of the direction, meaning and value of the change is sufficiently spread through large enough sections of the population of the world, it is indeed possible that the inevitable transformation will be much smoother and less marked by wholesale violence and catastrophic events.

PART ONE

I. THREE CENTURIES OF CRISIS

And the Discovery of Uranus, Neptune and Pluto

Today's most evident historical fact is that mankind has never known as rapid, intense and radical a period of change as during this and the two preceding centuries. The most similar period of transformation was no doubt that covering the first centuries B.C. and A.D., but it may be objected that this period had reference mainly to the Mediterranean world from which we have inherited our present European-American culture -- even though there were also basic changes occurring in India at the same time, especially the rise of a new form of Buddhism (Mahayana Buddhism) which was to spread fairly soon afterward to Tibet, China, and later Japan. Today, however, the crisis we are living through is global. Every continent and every human collectivity is affected by it, and indeed finds itself in a state of upheaval.

This fact must be given significance. If we believe in an ordered universe and an inherently structured process of human evolution, the historical fact must fit into a most important place in the pattern of cycles affecting the evolution not only of mankind, but of our entire earth -- if only for the reason that man today has presumably in his power to destroy most of life on this planet as well as to commit a global suicide. You cannot brush off these facts. We should make every conceivable attempt -- tentative and incomplete as these may prove to be in the eyes of men born five or ten centuries later -- to discover the meaning of the facts by situating them in time. And this means looking for relevant and illuminating clues wherever we can find them; even if it is difficult (or impossible indeed) to find clues which seem relevant and illuminating to e v e r y man and woman in our age of confusion, of undigested data and unintegrated intellectual disciplines.

To the astrologically minded person a most fascinating clue is given by the discovery of three until then (presumably) unknown planets in our solar system -- in the 18th century, Uranus, in the 19th century, Neptune, and in the 20th century, Pluto. It is easy to say that the reason why these planets were discovered is that man had perfected both new instruments (telescopes and sensitive photographic plates) and new intellectual methods (algebra, calculus, etc.). Both these instruments and these methods were needed to establish the presence of these distant planets, and of a variety of smaller celestial bodies in our solar system (mainly asteroids). But to say this simply transfers the significance from the cosmic to the intellectual level.

The discovery of Uranus, Neptune and Pluto is not mentioned here as the c a u s e of our world-crisis, but as the s y m b o l of its significance. What is particularly fascinating about it is that one can show that the over-all character of the basic changes which occurred during the 18th century -- at least in our Western culture which constituted the spearhead of evolutionary development at that time -- is truly "Uranian". Likewise the 19th century period (especially around the time of Neptune's discovery) is characteristically "Neptunian"; and the same is true of the connection between Pluto and our present century.

But how do we know what the terms Uranian, Neptunian and Plutonian signify? -- it will be asked. There are two ways of answering this question. Most astrologers would say that experience has proved that these newly discovered planets affect human beings or national and local events in definable ways; and that therefore each of these planets can be said to have a characteristic "nature" and "influence" upon human affairs, as a multitude of facts can easily prove. And this can hardly be denied by anyone who has carefully studied astrology for a few years.

However the answer I have given is that the solar system as a whole is an organized system in which the distance of a planet from the Sun establishes its essential character. This distance conditions the length of the planet's "period" (i. e. the time it takes to revolve around the Sun); and the solar system can be considered as a vast clock with many hands moving with different speeds and thus establishing cycles of greatly different lengths.

This, however, does not tell the whole story. Astrology, when we look closely at what it is able to interpret and give meaning to, appears as a symbolic language in which the structure in space and time of larger wholes (like the solar system) is related to the structural development of lesser wholes (an individual person, or humanity-as-a-whole). Astrology is indeed the practical application of a holistic philosophical approach to existence. According to this philosophy, every existential whole is contained within a greater whole which in turn is a lesser whole contained within a still greater whole. An organized system of existential activities is therefore both the container of lesser wholes, and one of the contents of a greater system. A molecule contains atoms, but is one of the many contents of a cell. A human being contains billions of cells and the human kingdom (or, more realistically, the planet Earth) contains billions of human beings.

This is a very fundamental principle in as much as it defines two spheres or realms of activity in any organized wholes. Any whole that we have ever observed can be said to have some sort of more or less central core -- because it originally emerged from some kind of "seed" or was integrated around a dynamic center (as for instance the void around which a whirling motion is formed). Most of the organized system normally is subject to the centripetal or gravitational pull of that core or integrating power; but there is also, at least in a potential and latent condition, a circumferential part of the whole which is affected by, and in due time becomes increasingly affected by the pull of the larger whole which totally surrounds and contains the smaller system.

A human being's activity is ruled originally and primarily by the central power of the life-energy within him, which we may call his self -- i. e. the particular rhythm of his own bio-psychic organism always seeking to maintain, preserve and reproduce itself. But no human being normally lives alone. He was at first member of a tribe, which constituted a most definite psychic (as well as biological and ethnic) whole living normally in a very defined geographical area -- even if that area was somewhat extensive in the case of nomadic pastoral groups. As member of this tribe he is controlled by specific loyalties; he obeys taboos and customs which define the basic rhythm of life of the community-as-a-whole. The tribesman is a lesser bio-psychic whole subjected to structural and quasi-instinctual forms of activity -- some of which may completely overcome his own rhythm and his drive for self-preservation and security.

Tribal communities become integrated into empires or modern nations; and a time almost inevitably will come when individual human beings will consider themselves as "lesser wholes" directly related without intermediaries to the "greater whole", Humanity -- and indeed to the entire planetary field of activities which we call the earth, the one "home" of all men at that level of consciousness. The pull of "Humanity" is indeed today affecting powerfully many individual persons, who dedicate their lives to "humanitarian" purposes (at one level or another) and are ready to sacrifice themselves for the sake of the formation of a "global" society structured by moral and legal principles.

If now we consider our solar system, we have reached a knowledge of astronomy enabling us to see this solar system as one of a multitude of such systems, or of various types of stellar organizations, contained within our vast galaxy. In terms of astrological symbolism -- if of nothing else that we as yet are able to know -- we may say, following the preceding line of reasoning, that the planets of our solar system may be divided into two groups. The planets up to and including Saturn are entirely under the influence of the gravitational power of the Sun, but the three newly discovered planets, Uranus, Neptune and Pluto, while still obeying this solar pull, are focal points through which the influence of the greater cosmic whole, the galaxy, is growing in power.

Every organized system of activity is subjected to two opposite pulls: centripetal force from the center of the system, and a centrifugal force which represents the urge to become related to and (in time) identified with the activities of the next "greater whole". In our solar system the actual boundaries within which the sun-ward centripetal pull is dominant are represented by Saturn, which, symbolically, is surrounded by a ring. Saturn, in the tradition of astrology, stands for the principle of limitation and of "form" in a particularistic and isolating sense. It refers to the principle of stability and security, to logic and to the ego that separates men while establishing their "name" and their inalienable social identity -- also to the skeleton which limits, but affirms, the structural character of the body. On the other hand, the planets beyond Saturn symbolize these forces in human nature (some would say beyond human nature) that impel men to reach beyond strictly defined, rational, exclusivistic modes of thinking, feeling and behavior.

I have spoken of Uranus, Neptune and Pluto figuratively as "ambassadors of the Galaxy" to our solar system. They are there, as it were, to show to whatever exists within the boundaries of Saturn a way out and beyond. They represent universalizing forces which forever tend to make of lesser wholes agents at the service of the greater Whole. In religious terms they may be said to symbolize the triune divinity latent in every man -- the divinity which at a certain time of growth and crisis in an individual's life may begin to challenge the pulls of the sun and the planets bound to the solar power, and eventually may come to be the dominant influence in the life of the man self-consecrated to so-called "spiritual" tasks. Such a consecration leads such a man (or woman) to follow a socially and culturally non-conforming course of action, because his mind and feelings have become repolarized and reoriented -- away from the sun and toward the galaxy, away from his ego and toward the welfare of humanity and an ever closer identification with whatever has structured and now guides the evolution of the earth and of Man.

The student of the many aspects of what has become known quite awkwardly, as "esoteric philosophy" -- or in terms of older religious traditions, mysticism -- speaks today of the "Path". To state that one is eager and ready to "enter upon the Path" means, in astrological symbolism, that one has become definitely responsive to energies which will increasingly bring men to a state of resonance to (and eventually of identification with) the broader rhythms of that vast cosmic Whole, the galaxy -- the realm of the stars. Uranus, Neptune and Pluto represent in such an operative symbolism the three basic phases of a process of repolarization and universalization of consciousness. We can visualize them as "stations" along this Path which leads man to the great "Initiation", as a result of which he becomes more-than-man, and (in religious terms) god-like.

What is implied in the concept of the Path is a dramatic increase in the speed of human evolution. This "steep and narrow" Path is often contrasted with the "highway of life" which is broad and open, and upon which the masses of mankind move slowly but mostly blindly in close togetherness, pushed by vast structural Forces acting within man as instinctual compulsions. An individual person on the Path is supposed to achieve in a relatively short time what humanity normally takes countless millennia to accomplish. However, there may be times during which the whole of humanity is stirred by an extraordinary ferment of growth, and during these dynamic times a relatively large number of individuals may come to maturity who feel powerfully the urge to begin this dangerous process of accelerated evolution. If their number is great enough they may polarize by their restless search and the tensions of their wills (and of their despairs also) the "descent" of super-planetary forces -- forces which we may interpret in religious terms as emanating from "God" or as powers inherent in the galaxy but at those times being focused in some unknown manner upon humanity (and perhaps upon the planet as a whole).

If Uranus, Neptune and Pluto are, symbolically at least, agents for the Galaxy they can be considered as "transformers" for the release of intense cosmic energies in a form acceptable to human beings, even if upheavals inevitably follow such a release. These "transformers" were evidently present in the solar system for millions of years, but they represented mostly latent possibilities as far as human consciousness was concerned. If they have been discovered and they have become integral parts of our conscious relationship to the universe during the last two centuries it is -- following this trend of reasoning -- because they had progressively flared up into intensified activity, rousing in at least the intellectual elite of mankind the capacity to become aware of their existence, thanks to the growth of new mental faculties.

It is for this reason that it is possible to say that humanity as a whole has been challenged to face the reality of this Path of accelerated evolution. This Path could lead to a kind of global Initiation IF the masses of mankind were able to resonate and respond positively and courageously to this downpour of galactic or divine energies; but will they be so able?

This is the question of questions.

If the opportunity is there, the knowledge of it and of what it really means should be spread widely all over the globe; for this Path of Initiation (or total human metamorphosis) must be trodden c o n s c i o u s l y. It is indeed the "Conscious Way" of evolution. It requires a well developed and structured mind, able to rise above all emotional attachments to events and to find its security and its strength in its attunement to cycles and structural factors -- and first of all in a deep realization of individual destiny (as I defined this term).

It should therefore be very important to understand what the planets Uranus, Neptune and Pluto may represent in an operative, cosmic and dynamic sense, and in any case what they stand for in the symbolic language (the "algebra") of astrology. And here we are confronted with the striking fact, already mentioned, that what these planets indicate when they are especially activated in the birth-chart of individual persons (by natal aspects, and by transits) can be very significantly related to the basic character of the respective centuries during which they became c o n s c i o u s   f a c t o r s in   the   c o l l e c t i v e   m i n d   of   M a n.   Indeed it helps greatly the astrologically aware mind in its attempt to understand the meaning of the 18th, 19th and 20th centuries, as periods of history filled with transforming events, to relate them respectively to Uranus, Neptune and Pluto. Even if considered only as symbols of structural characteristics, these planets throw some more significant light on what has happened to our Western civilization since 1700. They help us to s i t u a t e our place in a vast planetary all-human process of transformation in which we are compelled willy nilly to participate -- whether ours be a positive or a negative participation; whether we are reaching toward galactic spaces or falling back in fear and inertia to the realm bounded by Saturnian formations, social-cultural and personal.

The enemies of all radical transformations powered by the energies focused through Uranus, Neptune and Pluto are, on the one hand, the pair of the largest planets of the solar system, Jupiter and Saturn -- and on the other hand, the pair of planets closest to the Earth, Mars and Venus. Jupiter and Saturn represent the social and religious level of human existence, and all that relates to institutions and to the power wielded by the men who control them. Jupiter, psychologically speaking, refers to the social sense, the realization that "united we win, isolated we lose" in the struggle for survival and increased comfort, and, at its deeper level, to the religious feeling which is an extension of the social sense and the drive toward. unity. Saturn is, as we already have seen, the feeling of security which comes from officially recognized participation in a steady system of organization which guarantees you exclusive right to your name, your place, your status, your possessions. Saturn is therefore always opposing the urge for radical self-transformation and social-cultural changes which upset the status quo at any level, which challenge the Establishment and its particular, exclusivistic type of law and order.

Mars and Venus, being the planets on either side of the Earth, stand for what is most personal and intimate in an individual's life and temperament. These factors usually develop within the social-cultural structures represented by Jupiter and Saturn, yet they can also withdraw from subservience to the community and unfold on a strictly individual basis. They can also eventually be repolarized and become transfigured by experiences which belong to the realm of the trans-Saturnian planets -- but if the individual should fail in his attempt at treading the Path of transformation, and the energies represented by Uranus, Neptune and particularly Pluto have become in him negative and anarchistic, then Venus may refer to a total perversion of human values, and Mars to an equally perverted and sadistic lust for violence.

If we now consider European history during the last centuries we can significantly say that the classical century of Louis XIV ("The State it is I" -- i.e. ego-glorification) has all the characteristics of Saturn, socially and culturally. Versailles is the perfect symbol of a courtly, aristocratic and utterly formalistic society. Louis XIV was called le Roi-soleil (the Sun-King), but Saturn and the sun are closely linked, as circumference and center are linked. It is against the concepts of "kingship by divine right" and of a union of Church and State (Jupiter and Saturn welded into one unit), and against social privileges, Church dogmatism and the cosmic mechanism of a Descartes, that the Uranian 18th century fought. The fight was led by Free-Masonry (with its ideal of comradeship of work and fraternity of soul), by the French Encyclopedists and their relentless criticisms of the Medieval mentality, by the Revolutionary Movements in America and in France.

Under these Uranian assaults and in the search for a principle of order more universal than that of the Classical era, the Neptunian quality of feeling emerged already toward the close of the 18th century in the glorification, by Jean-Jacques Rousseau, of "human nature" and in a strong belief among the new philosophers and scientists of the day in "natural law" as a substitute for a particular system of "revealed" religion and ethics. This trend developed into Romanticism and led to humanitarianism, French religious socialism, the Communist Manifesto, and the start of the first attempt at organizing on the basis of a "Divine Manifestation" a truly global "World Order" -- the Bahai Movement. This great religious Movement, whose initial phase began in 1844 in Persia with the message of an extraordinary Personage, the Bab, (soon put to death by the Saturnian Mohammedan clergy) grew in power under his successor, Baha'u'-llah, whom several millions of adherents to the Faith, organized in communities throughout every continent, regard as the Messenger of God and Law-Giver for the New Age -- that Age so widely expected today everywhere as "the Aquarian Age".

The Industrial Revolution, based on the power of steam

and later oil, is a Neptunian phenomenon. It d i s s o l v e d what the power represented by Uranus had shattered and broken through. Yet every action of the universalizing forces has a reaction; and it tends to crystallize under the inertial resistance to change of Saturn-based privileges. The universalizing Neptunian forces stopped before reaching the whole globe, and manifested as the drive toward strong nations extending their influence around the globe by means of colonialism; and, as the aristocrats of the old European order had regained considerable power after the Napoleonic wars, they soon cornered the new energies released by the Industrial Revolution. At the opposite pole of society a new class of human beings, the Proletariat, became the field for the Neptunian forces which tend to level down and reduce every differentiated structure to a kind of liquid and amorphous chaos.

Neptune is the Universal Solvent of the Alchemists. It is the deep fog which rises from melting icebergs and covers the seashore. It refers to all kinds of "navigation" over large expanses of space, be these oceanic, or today atmospheric or stratospheric; and navigation links all seemingly separate continents and politically differentiated nations, building a vast and ever-expanding network of communications. These serve as lines of force upon which a future global society can be built. They also bring about "melting pot" conditions and what the old Hindus called the "confusion of castes".

As we shall see presently, in 1891-92 Neptune and Pluto met in the sky at the beginning of the zodiacal sign, Gemini -- sign of the intellect and of the communion of minds. Gradually this Plutonian factor began to press forward from the collective unconscious of mankind into public recognition (19-30). World War I with its static confrontations in the wet and muddy battle fields of France and with its poison gas was still a Neptunian kind of war, allowing even for the glamor of being "the war to end all wars" -- for Neptune is essentially related to glamor. Glamor in all its manifestations,

is the lure which impels men to venture into the unknown
with glowing faith, and to take steps ahead which they would
never take if they knew rationally and objectively what is
ahead. Love too is a glamor thrown by life over the meeting
of boys and girls to make them forget, at least temporarily,
their separated egocentric thinking and planning. And there
is also the glamor which veils and glorifies the hard and
tedious facts and duties of mother -- and the glamor of religious devotion to a transcendent God dwelling far above the
clouds of human frailty which may drive men to asceticism
or martyrdom.

As Pluto became sighted and it entered the field of consciousness of mankind, Fascism and Nazism began to rise
to world-importance, and the Electronic (or Technological)
Revolution, announced by the discovery of X-rays, radium
and the Quantum Theory after Neptune had met Pluto, began
to affect an ever-increasing area of our modern society. Uranus shatters the Saturnian past by the lightning power of a
new vision; and it releases "seed ideas" which sooner or later germinate in the minds of a few pioneers, then condition
the intellectual processes of the vanguard of humanity. Neptune loosens and if possible dissolves what Uranus has shattered, and this includes man's sense of security and his allegiance to obsolescent institutions. Pluto then pulverizes
whatever is left standing, reducing everything of the past to
a kind of undifferentiated state.

However, what finds itself in this nearly undifferentiated
condition at first desperately craves some semblance of
the cohesion it used to know. As a result it tends to aggre-
gate into various kinds of whirlpools formed by the power of
some hurricane-like energy. The "Fuehrer"-Leader appears
in answer to the subconscious yearning of the mass mind for
solidity; but the solidity it gains -- that of the totalitarian
Party or of the gang in modern slums -- is deceiving and always ends in violence (physical or psychological) and often
in catastrophy. Pluto may be a symbol of death, but at first

of a death that does not want to die, and haunts the weak, empty minds of individuals or collectivities, driving them to seek the bitter satisfaction of dis-humanized greed and lust, and to crime or collective psychic and economic vampirism.

Yet Pluto is also, in its positive aspect, the principle of re-ordering and rebirth inherent in all seeds. It is the gates to immortality; which means the ability for an individual, or a special group (the Biblical "remnant"), to retain its identity -- at least on the level of the mind -- while all else decays under the relentless pressure of the closing cycle. Pluto symbolizes the Universal Brotherhood of Man in seed; but for those millions of human beings who refuse to or actually cannot become consciously integrated in this "seed" the alternative is perhaps an experience of all-human unity through the mixing of bloods on gory battlefields, or the mixing of ashes in the vast whirlpools which a widespread nuclear holocaust would generate, blotting out the sun and destroying or perverting much of life on earth.

Shall man discover -- perhaps at the beginning of the 21st century -- another planet beyond Pluto? The existence of such a planet has been considered probable by some astronomers; and some astrologers, in America and Europe, have not only calculated the general orbit it may have, but have spoken of several more distant planets. Their existence is not at all impossible; but my feeling is that only one planet is to be soon discovered beyond Pluto, and many years ago I have spoken of it -- as a hypothesis -- giving it the name Proserpine. (Dutch astrologers have used instead the Greek name, Persephone). If it does exist it would naturally and logically be the symbol of concrete rebirth after the threefold crisis on the Path of transformation. It would signify the foundation of a new type of human existence in which the dualism of life and death would be transcended by a consciousness able to experience cyclically both without loss of identity -- a condition relating to the great myth of the goddess Proserpine who passed a third of her existence with

Pluto in the "Underworld" and the other two thirds on the Earth's surface, as a symbol of a reborn vegetation. Proserpine would then represent the mind of the Initiate who, like the Lazarus of the Gospel, has known death and is resurrected through the power of a divine Being, his "Master" or guru.

Regardless of such a possibility, the fact is that we are dealing now with three planets beyond Saturn which indeed should be regarded as a unit, i.e. as a trinity -- if for no other reason than the lengths of their periods of revolution around the Sun are related in a most unusual manner. The period of Neptune is twice, and that of Pluto three times the length of the period of Uranus. Such a 1-2-3 relationship between the time-cycles of successive planets is unique in our solar system; and any fact that is thus singled out must be given a special significance in any gestalt and therefore in any system of symbolism.

Thus, the correlation between Uranus, Neptune and Pluto and the three basic century-long phases of the process of total reorganization of humanity corresponding to their official discovery becomes even more meaningful. We are led to assume that the three planets constitute a real "trinity" of aspects -- the three aspects of one single process of transformation of the deepest implications of human existence. We see this process at work in individual persons as we study the trans-Saturnian planets and their transits in relation to individual birth-charts; and we are shown in a measurable way how such processes operate in the lives of modern persons. In the past these processes were considered "occult" and they involved the greatest secrecy and awe-inspiring tests; but since Uranus, Neptune and Pluto have, as it were, come out from the unconscious depths of man's inner being and entered the consciousness of at least the evolutionary spearhead of humanity, the Mysteries of the past are being "dis-occulted".

When the human mentality was formed under the rigid

patterns of social-cultural systems of communal organization celestially dominated by Jupiterian religions and Saturnian rites and dogmas, everything that would transcend and
could lead to the universalization of the worshipped Tradition was publicly taught to be evil, and only made known, in
the secrecy of some Holy of Holies, to selected and harshly
tested candidates to Initiation.   But now that the t r a n s -
S a t u r n i a n planets have entered the conscious Mind of Humanity, the radical crises of consciousness to which modern
man is subjected -- as his most fundamental bio-psychic al-
legiances are being dissolved into meaninglessness -- have
taken the place of the greater part of what once was occulted.
M o d e r n l i f e i t s e l f i s t h e t e s t e r because this life
challenges us to make crucial decisions that only a few selected and trained individuals could make in the past.

We can indeed validly assume that mankind is in the midst
of a process of extensive "mutation" -- a fundamental change
in consciousness; and the fact that Uranus, Neptune and Pluto
have entered the field of human consciousness is, I believe,
an evident and powerful symbol of the spread of this process
to an ever larger section of mankind. This does n o t imply that the process will be a success, or that the mutation
will not have a great many destructive and regressive results. Whether it will or not, how much greater the over-
all success will be than the inevitable failures, and how
changed -- and probably much diminished in number -- humanity will be at the end of our global crisis: these are questions to which no valid answers can be given today. I do not
seek to prophecize, but only to elucidate.

II. PLANETARY CYCLES

And the Ten-Thousand Year Period

If as students of astrology we attempt to discover the basic rhythm structuring the periodical transformations of human societies and civilizations, which in turn reflect as well as concretize fundamental changes in the consciousness of the vanguard of mankind, we have to look for such a rhythm first of all in the periodical motions of the slower and most distant planets, Uranus, Neptune and Pluto. These planets have been related in the preceding chapter to the crucial transformation of human living conditions and social-cultural values during the last centuries. We are today, it seems evident, reaching toward the last phase of this at least tentative mutation in Man's consciousness, and the three trans-Saturnian planets have become integral parts of the collective mind of humanity, each during the century whose overall character was most like the planet's own character as a potent and verifiable symbol of processes of transformation.

This evidently did not mean, I repeat, that the planets were not dynamic factors in this great Field of cosmic activity, the solar system, before man knew publicly of their presence and their potential of symbolic and effective meaning. They were present in the sub-conscious background of human consciousness, and the cycles defined and structured by their revolutions around the Sun were operative factors in the evolution of mankind and of civilization. These cycles, as we saw, display a remarkable relationship, as Pluto's mean period of revolution (245.33 years) is about three times that of Uranus' period (83.75 years) which is very near the half of Neptune's period (163.74 years).*

---

*These are periods in the *tropical* zodiac which is used as the basis of calculations and interpretations in this book. The periods are naturally a

These periods are not e x a c t l y in a 1.2.3 relationship but the very interesting and no doubt most significant fact is that we do not find in the universe or in the earth's biosphere any relationship between life-periods or cycles which produces exact numbers. The same thing is true of the shapes of living organisms and presumably of celestial systems; for while we can definitely speak of spiral forms in growth processes, of the geometrical patterns of leaves, etc., these shapes are probably never e x a c t l y perfect in a geometrical sense. The geometrical forms abstracted by man's rational mind are "archetypes" of living or cosmic processes; they are ideal Images. In the actual world of existence forms and cycles only approximate these archetypes, because in this existential world the infinite multiplicity of relationships between all existents introduces unceasingly slight variations and modifications.

This is why ancient philosophers spoke of a "World of Formation" as it were behind or above our world of earthly existence -- the world of perfect archetypes, which was seen also to be the expression of the Mind of God, the Great Architect of the Universe. In terms of our actual existential experience no cycle is exactly twice the length of another; and we have the same thing in musical theory. Twelve intervals of fifths (a 3 to 2 relationship) cover a little more than seven octaves (a 2 to 1 relationship) -- and this "more" is known as the Pythagorean comma. It is by taking out a twelfth part of this very small comma interval from every one of the twelve fifths that we have the exactly even intervals of half-tones in the modern type of "equal temperament".

This musical example has a great deal of relevance to our present discussion, for twelve revolutions of Uranus ar-

---

little shorter than the ones in the *sidereal* zodiac which, for some unknown reason are given in the current astrological ephemerides, though the latter use positions in the tropical zodiac. (The figures given here were obtained from Charles Jayne, of his articles in N. de Yore *Encyclopedia of Astrology.)*

ound the sun add up to a little over 1000 years; and this 1000 year cycle -- and also the nearly 500-year cycle established by the successive conjunctions of Neptune and Pluto, of which more presently -- constitute basic time measures, according to old occult traditions. Four periods of Pluto last presumably about 981½ years, and six periods of Neptune 982.44 years. I say "presumably" for it may be naive to think that we know the e x a c t lengths of these periods over a long span of years, and changes in the pattern of the solar system certainly should not be ruled out, as all planetary orbits have a remarkable way of being affected by the vast complexity of gravitational influences, and perhaps by other even more powerful factors.

Actually it seems that the most significant over-all period, if we consider the general evolution of human civilization, is the 10,000 year period, which is a little over 40 cycles of Pluto, 60 cycles of Neptune and over 120 cycles of Uranus. Again these are "archetypal" measures, for various factors enter into the picture, and if we think of such periods in relation to a planet's zodiacal position the question of whether we speak of the sidereal or the tropical zodiac cannot be avoided. What we are trying to ascertain when using these large cycles is not exact dates at which some spectacular events occur, but the r h y t h m and the s t r u c t u r a l p a t t e r n s of evolutionary processes with regard to our planet, Earth. We are thinking as "generalists" not as technicians-specialists. We are trying to understand even more than to "know"; and there is a kind of knowledge -- very much favored today -- which runs counter to understanding. One must know certain basic principles in order to understand; but the quality and the intent of so much of our modern scientific knowledge precludes a deep, general understanding of what is known, because the knowledge is tendencious and hypnotized by technological considerations and by the demand that it should be immediately applicable, socially productive and renumerative to those who finance

the research. This quite definitely applies to some recent
attempts made to "prove scientifically" the validity of astrology.

The 10,000 year cycle was mentioned at the close of my
book, THE ASTROLOGY OF PERSONALITY (page 526, 19-
35) and it was pointed out that, according to the Teachers of
H. P. Blavatsky, it refers to the periodical manifestation --
in and through a particular human personage -- of the Bud-
dha-Principle; that is, of what one might call the Universal Mind. One can think of such manifestations as the focusing upon our planet of the cosmic Principle of Wholeness
that sustains and integrates the immense rhythms of the galaxy in which our solar system operates as a small and not
too central unit. The significant fact, however, is that such
a 10,000 year cycle seems to be related to evolutionary and
historical turning points of great importance, and that it
makes of the very last years of the 19th century one of these
crucial turning points.

The most definite date related to this cycle is the date
which marked, in the great tradition of India, the beginning
of the Kali Yuga (the Greek Iron Age) -- a long dark period,
but also the period during which what one should call the
"gestation process" of a new and infinitely more spiritually
conscious humanity is taking place; Kali refers to the mo-
ther-principle. The date is 3102 B.C. Around 1898 A.D.
the first five thousand years of Kali Yuga ended. Ten thous-
and years before this recent date brings us to 8102 B.C.
which, according to the old Egyptian tradition was the time
of the sinking of the last great island in the Atlantic Ocean
which once had been part of the fabled continent of Atlantis.

If this were a correct hypothesis, we might say that this
final disappearance of the "Atlanteans" marked the beginning, or just preceded the beginning, of a new wave of civilization, a new 10,000 year cycle. The diagram which follows shows how such a cycle could be divided. The 3102
B.C. beginning of the Kali Yuga would be the polarizing point

of the cycle -- the "result" of what had begun 5000 years before. The quartering of the cycle into four 2500 year periods produces most significant dates. 5602 B.C. would probably refer to the earliest Persian civilization and to the Cretan-Hellenic culture which reached its apex in Greece in 602 B.C. During the sixth century B.C. Gautama the Buddha and other great spiritual Teachers lived, who sowed the seed for a deep-seated transformation of the Mind of humanity, a transformation which reached a "critical state" around 1900 A.D. with the discovery of radio-activity and the start of the Electronic (or Atomic) Age.

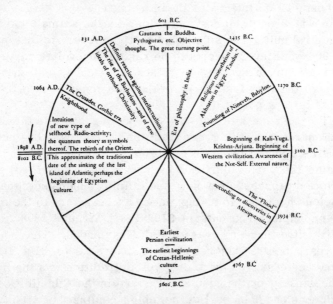

Dividing the 10,000 year cycle into twelve sub-periods gives also significant spans, relating to important changes in human civilization, particularly the periods following 231 A.D. (the rise of "the Barbarians") and 1064 A.D. (the Crusades); both dates mark the decisive starts of processes that altered the character of "Western" civilization. We shall see in the next chapters how these periods dovetail in with other cycles and sub-cycles produced by considering not only the nearly 500-year long Neptune-Pluto conjunction-cycle, but the nearly 26,000 year long cycle of the precession of the equinoxes, with its twelve component "Ages".

That the 10,000 year cycle contains 40 periods of Pluto and 60 periods of Neptune is a fact that will interest anyone acquainted with the traditional significance of the numbers 40 and 60. The number 40 refers to the 40 weeks of pregnancy, and it has been associated with periods of incubation, of spiritual preparation and/or of tests (40 years of wandering in the desert by the group led by Moses; the 40 years of imprisonment in Akka -- meaning "womb" -- of Abdul Baha, son of the great Bahai Prophet, Baha'u'llah; the 40 days of Lent; and also the yearly 40 days of hibernation of the bear, spoken of in alchemical texts -- the bear symbolizing a form of cosmic power, and of course most important extra-zodiacal constellations.) As Pluto represents, in its deepest meaning, the process of formation of a new, higher and more permanent entity within an earth-born organism -- i.e. its "seed" -- the connection between this planet and the number 40 is significant. I might even add, for numerologically oriented readers, that Pluto's discovery was announced in 19-30. Adding the digits of that year gives us 13, which reduces to 4 -- plus a zero; thus 40.

The number 60 is also very significant in association with the higher meaning of Neptune. Marc Edmund Jones wrote (in his course SYMBOLICAL ASTROLOGY) that "The number 60 is the Babylonian or Solar Mysteries solvent of all problems"; and the planet Neptune is also in its deepest meaning the Universal Solvent of all that is in bondage to particular forms and egocentric structures. The number 60 refers also to the period measured by three conjunctions of Jupiter and Saturn after which the two planets return to their starting point (with a few degrees of difference) in the zodiac; and it was this Jupiter-Saturn cycle which was most

prominently used in ancient "mundane astrology" related to
social processes, affairs of State, etc.

Today the concept of closely knit social-political organization within definite boundaries is being superseded -- in
terms of our recent attempts at some kind of f e d e r a l world-
organization open to all men, national groups and races --
by a Neptunian all-embracing ideal. Neptune is also the symbol of compassion, of the Mystic Body of Christ. It refers
to the "living Water" which surrounds and protects the em-
bryonic growth of the New Humanity that is to be. The 60
periods of Neptune represent thus a basic phase in the unfoldment of this ideal condition of mankind -- the still far
distant true "Millennium" which is more likely to refer to a
hundred thousand years (or more) than to a mere thousand
years.

WHEN DOES A URANUS CYCLE BEGIN?

The 10,000 year period includes 120 Uranus cycles, plus
one extra period of nearly 84 years which can be considered
significantly as a "seed-period" linking two 10,000 year cycles. It would have about the same meaning as the above-
mentioned Pythagorean comma in music -- i.e. the amount
by which a cyclic series of 12 fifths is greater than 7 octaves. Indeed Uranus can be related symbolically to the musical interval of the fifth (C to G), because this interval is
the foundation of the process of "modulation" from one ton-
ality to another. Likewise Uranus represents essentially
the power enabling man to ascend from one level of consciousness to the next: that is, to experience a true metamorphosis. Astrologers know well how closely the transits of
Uranus over the Sun, the Moon, the four Angles, etc. of a
natal chart relate to crisis of changes which (if all goes well!)
enable the person to reach a new level of consciousness.
Thus in the 10,000 year cycle, Uranus' periods constitute,
as it were, the minute hand of the clock of evolution on this
Earth.

Uranus moves every seven years into a new sign of the zodiac -- and the seven-year cycle is probably the most important period in the unfoldment of a thinking individual person. Four such cycles (or 28 years) mark the length of the three great periods of a human life having reached the stage of at least relative individualization; and today we are fast approaching the time when we shall see the life-span of a fully developed individual averaging 84 years, a complete revolution of Uranus around the Sun.

The typical Great Cycle of Uranus encompasses thus about 1005 years and witnesses 144 times the passage of Uranus into a new zodiacal sign; and we recall the use of this number 144 in Biblical symbolism. An analysis of this 1005 year cycle will reveal very interesting and historically relevant connections between the beginning of each of the 12 periods and important changes in the process of civilization.

However the problem we are facing here, as in all similar cyclic measuring, is how to select a valid starting point for the cycle. Two logical possibilities can be considered:

(1) the 84 year long Uranus cycle could be said to begin when Uranus passes from South to North declination. This corresponds to what happens at the spring equinox, when the Sun crosses the celestial equator moving northward -- and this crossing marks the beginning of the astrological year, and of various calendars past and present. Such a passage into North declination by Uranus occurs theoretically around the time this planet has longitude $0°$ (i.e. Aries $0°$). However, while the passage of the Sun from south to north declination is clear-cut and happens only once every yearly cycle, the crossing of the celestial equator by planets such as Uranus, Neptune and Pluto gives rise to an ambiguous situation. The planet oscillates back and forth from south to north, then to south again and north declination. This occurs also, in reverse order, when the planet moves from north to south declination; so that, for instance, Uranus will move from south to north declination at the end of

March 1969 while it is retrograding in Libra after having moved from north to south declination late in October 1968.

This produces such an ambiguous situation that it seems far more sensible to use, for the purpose of a broad study of the Uranus cycle the time when Uranus reaches only once every cycle Aries 0° by heliocentric measurement. This happened for the last time in the spring 1927. This was the time of Lindbergh's solo flight across the Atlantic. U.S. marines had just landed in Nicaragua and in China. French Premier Briand's activities were aiming at a European Federation, while in Germany Hitler was gradually building a strong Nazi organization. Pluto was officially discovered in 1929-1930.

(2) The Uranus cycle begins when the planet reaches its North Node (heliocentric), moving from a South to a North latitude. Uranus' North Node is at present at about 13°50' Gemini; and according to recent ephemerides moving forward at the rate of 18 seconds of arc per year, which means half a degree per century. (Old astronomical works gave different figures and suggested periods during which some of the planets' nodes were retrograde. Hindu treatises speak of planetary nodes cycles lasting several hundred of thousand years).

The last heliocentric passage of Uranus over its North Node occurred most significantly on July 20, 1945, four days after the first atomic explosion in Alamagordo, N.M. which indeed ushered in a new era -- for better or for worse. The previous crossing of the ecliptic from South to North declination occurred in June, 1861 just after the inauguration of Lincoln and the start of the Civil War -- also the beginning of modern Italy as a kingdom under Victor-Emmanuel, the Mexican Expedition by France, England and Spain, and important events in China and Japan. Another crossing occurred in 1777 during the War of Independence; and in 1693, 1609 and 1526.

The nodes of a planet are the two ends of the line of int-

ersection between two planes, the plane of the earth's orbit
(the ecliptic or zodiac) and the plane of that planet's orbit.
The planetary nodes are thus heliocentric factors; or more
significantly stated, they are produced by the interactions
between the whorls of activity generated by the planet's and
the earth's motions around the common focus of their two
elliptical orbits. From our terrestrial point of view these
interactions have been given a twofold or bi-polar valuation.
The north node brings to a focus the more positive or active
aspect of the planet in its relation to our earth and its humanity. The south node, on the other hand, focalizes the
basic reaction of the earth and of men to the other planet's
activity.

In our present historical period, the north node of Uranus
being in mid-Gemini, the creative and transforming a c t i o n
of Uranus upon earth-life and the planetary mind of Man is
focused at the Gemini level of intellectual activity. Man's
reaction is focused in Sagittarius. Thus the Uranian factor
in human consciousness and behavior takes often the form of
an expansive and at times fanatic or at least religious and
self-righteous activity. The interesting thing in the Sagittarius rising chart for the American p e o p l e (as differentiated from the American G o v e r n m e n t) is that the most
likely Ascendant is at about 13° Sagittarius, thus very close
to the South Node of Uranus. For a multitude of reasons
which I have discussed in many articles and lectures, this
Ascendant and the Libra 2° Mid Heaven fit remarkably well
the American character and typical way of life ("the abund-
ant life" with a golf course in every center of population!)
The U.S. as a whole embodies the r e a c t i o n s of Western
man to the Uranian forces released creatively in Europe
since the Renaissance -- and before in Greece. These Uranian forces within restless Europeans who had been frustrated by the old feudal structures of the Middle Ages found
in the "virgin soil" of America a fertile field for their unparalleled development. But what we witness here are re-

sults, much more than initiating causes. Relatively very few new inventions were really "discovered" in America, i.e. discovered as transforming ideas in the creative mind of Man. They were "applied" here by remarkable technological intellects expert in management and in making opportune and daring executive decisions.

In the U.S. chart with a Gemini Ascendant, Uranus is rising in the first House; and the majority of astrologers still consider this a characteristic expression of American inventiveness, yearning for change and restlessness or rootlessness. But I have come to realize that the Uranus character is even more marked -- and more fatefully marked -- when the horizon of a birth-chart is practically identical with Uranus' lines of nodes, than when Uranus, the planet, is rising. The rising planet suggests that the person will discover his true nature and character through Uranian events and activities; but when the natal horizon is identical to the line of Uranus' nodes there is an absolutely basic, karmic or structural identification between the person's individuality and Uranus. Indeed the individual person is born indelibly stamped with Uranus' power, and fated to act as a transforming force in society, as an "agent" of Uranus.

But, to return to the problem of what constitutes the most valid starting point of the 84-year Uranus cycle: it seems logical to say that, if one seeks information about these transforming forces and pressures which refer to Uranus considered in themselves, one should consider the passage of the planet over its north node as the relevant point -- and this would be true in any planet's case. However, if one seeks to establish the larger rhythms of the solar system as a whole, as these affect our earth and especially the biosphere in which all living organisms interact, are born and die, then it seems best to use the equinoxes as the basic starting point of everything.

At the equinoxes the sun moves from south to north, and north to south declination as it crosses the celestial

equator -- an extension of the earth's equator plane. The
sun has never any celestial latitude; for celestial latitude is
measured north or south of the ecliptic's plane, which is the
plane of the sun's apparent yearly motion (i.e. the plane of
the earth's orbit in modern astronomy.) "Solar" values --
from the geocentric point of view -- are fundamental whenever the whole solar system is considered in its effect upon
life on earth. Thus declination is more important in this
sense than celestial latitude.

However, the orbit of every planet is an ellipse, not a
circle; and an ellipse has two foci, instead of one center.
All planetary orbits have one c o m m o n   f o c u s, at which
the sun stands; but each planetary orbit has also its own independent focus. This focus symbolizes the planet's individual character; and we might also infer that the latitude cycle of each planet expecially refers to the development of
this individual character -- or more exactly it represents
the process by which the energies symbolized by the planet
affect life on this Earth.

When Uranus passed over its north node in 1945 the first
uranium-powered atomic bomb was released. This was a
strictly Uranian event with vast consequences for the Earth's
biosphere and all men. But this event was part of a larger
pattern of global transformation for mankind, and this pattern began to be clearly revealed earlier when Hitler, released from prison, emerged as the future leader of aggres-
sive Nazi Germany. This emergence occurred around the
year 1927 when Uranus reached heliocentrically the first degree of Aries -- and it began to have a north declination (19-
27-28).

THE "GREAT CYCLE" OF URANUS
As already stated, 12 revolutions of Uranus around its
orbit last a little over 1000 years -- a millennium. Because
of this fact, and in analogy with the solar year with its 12
zodiacal signs, one might speak of this millennial period as

the "Great Year" of Uranus. The most important turning-points in such a "Great Year" are quite evidently its beginning and mid-point which correspond to the equinoctial points of the solar year. The transforming impulse of the beginning finds its apex and concrete manifestation at the mid-point, somewhat too as the impulse originating at a New Moon finds its fulfillment (or else begins to break down) at the Full Moon.

But one could also, perhaps even more significantly, compare this Great Cycle of about 1000 years to the transits of Uranus through the twelve Houses of an astrological chart; also, musicologists with a philosophical-occult bend of mind could establish an analogy with the series of twelve intervals of fifths which encompass nearly the entire span of a piano keyboard. Thus in what follows I shall simply refer to twelve "phases" of the Great Cycle.

The interesting fact is that, if we start around the time of the beginning of Kali Yuga according to the already mentioned Hindu tradition, this Uranian "Great Year" gives us very significant turning points, and leads us to the conclusion that the beginning of the current 84-year cycle of Uranus in 1927 was the start of a millennial "Great Year".

From 1927, going past-ward, we reach 922 A. D. which was the real beginning of the great Medieval culture in a Europe spiritually united by the Church, its chain of monasteries, and its "universal" language, Latin. Another 1005 years before, we come to near 84 B. C. which may be very close to the beginning of what is called the Piscean Age, which we shall presently study. Rome was in civil war and engaged in a bloody war against Mithridates in Asia Minor. Greece was falling to Rome and Caesar was a child.

The preceding Great Cycle had begun around 1089 B. C. which seems to be about the start of the archaic Greek culture, of Tyre, and of the process that led to the establishment of the short-lived Hebrew Kingdom. The 2094 B. C. period is that of the great days of Babylon (Hammurabi) and of the Theban period in Egypt; and another millennium brings us just about the 3102 B.C. date of the Kali Yuga, and of the early Egyptian dynasties in Memphis.

The mid-phase of the Great Cycle 1089 to 84 B.C. comes at the time of Gautama the Buddha, of Lao Tzu, Pythagoras, and other great spiritual leaders. It follows the destruction of the Assyrian Empire by the Medes; it sees the rise of the new Babylon, the captivity of Israel, the rise of a new Persian Empire.

The mid-phase of the Great Cycle from 84 B.C. to 1005 A.D. witnessed in 410 A.D. the sacking of Rome by the Barbarians, a Greek revival of civilization in Persia and the Near East -- and the invasion of Europe by the Huns (defeated in 451 A.D. at Chalons, France).

The following cycle's mid-phase brings us to 1424 A.D., Joan of Arc and the birth of nationalism, the invention of printing, the beginning of Humanism, prelude to the Renaissance.

The beginning of the Christian era corresponds very closely to the second phase (i. e. twelfth part) of the Great Cycle which began in 84 B. C.; the tenth phase witnesses the enormous extension of Islam and the conquest by the Arabs of North Africa, Spain, etc. The eleventh phase sees the rise of the Carolingian Kings in France, Charlemagne who became emperor -- and the apex of Arab civilizaition. The twelfth phase witnesses the Treaty of Verdun (843) which divides Charlemagne's empire and establishes the karmic pattern upon which the West European civilizaiton will develop.

The third ("Gemini") phase of the following Great Cycle (922 to 1927 A. D.) begins with the First Crusade, with the earliest development of universities (Abelard in Paris) and of polyphonic music. The sixth ("Virgo") phase witnessed the Hundred Years War between France and England, the "Black Death" which killed a vast amount of people -- while

Tamerlane revived the Mogol Empire.

The eighth ("Scorpio") phase began soon after Columbus' "discovery" of America. It witnessed the Reformation and religious wars -- but also the Renaissance. The ninth phase corresponds to the late Elizabethan Age, with Francis Bacon and Shakespeare. As the tenth phase began in 1676 A. D. Louis XIV and "classicism" dominated the European stage; but the seed of a new era were sown in England and France. Free Masonry began in London in 1717. Peter the Great modernized Russia, and Frederick the Great built a strong Prussia.

The eleventh ("Aquarius") phase (1760-1844) witnessed the Seven Years' War and later the Revolutionary era. Uranus was discovered in 1781. The Napoleonic Era and the subsequent political Reaction followed. The new technology and idealistic form of socialism (Fourier, St. Simon, Robert Owen, etc.) were being developed.

The twelfth phase was indeed karmic, and yet a prelude to our present era of technology and global wars. The Bahai Movement was announced in 1844. The Communist Manifesto and Revolutionary movements began in 1848; and this Great Cycle ended with the rise of Japan, with World War I -- and the growth of Soviet Communism.

The Great Cycle starting in 1927 was soon followed by the Great Depression; and in spite of Aristide Briand's and a few other great Europeans' efforts to build a federal Europe World War II was being prepared. We are living now at the mid-point of the first phase of this new 1005 year period. This phase will end in 2011 A. D. Uranus has entered the sign Libra -- and deep changes are impending as I write these pages, particularly in the United States whose "birthchart" (I repeat) has Libra 2^0 as its Mid-Heaven.

Knowing this may help us to pin-point our position insofar as the processes which refer to the transformation and reorientation of our present-day society are concerned. A new cycle of Uranian changes has already begun; but this

cycle must not be confused with the "Aquarian Age" of which
we shall soon speak, though in a sense the Uranian cycle is
announcing, preparing the way and next century will blend
with the twice as long Aquarian Age.

THE CYCLE OF NEPTUNE

Six Neptunian revolutions around the Sun last about 982.74
years; thus it enters 71 times a new sign of the zodiac. Neptune reached heliocentrically Aries 0^0 at the end of August
1861. The geocentric transit occurred for the first time on
April 13th, 1861 exactly when the fall of Fort Sumter marked
the beginning of the Civil War -- quite a "coincidence"! Neptune went back briefly into Pisces and re-entered Aries on
February 14, 1862 when two forts surrendered to the Union
forces of General Grant (born in 1822 near the time Pluto
entered Aries). The surrender of forts -- i.e. of Saturnian
enclosures -- symbolize interestingly the beginnings of the
present Neptune cycle. Neptune was then in "transforming"
quintile aspect to Uranus.

The preceding cycle began in 1697-98, with Neptune in
square to Uranus entering Capricorn.* This was the cycle
which witnessed the collapse of the old order in Europe. The
Neptune-cycle beginning in 1861 will end in 2025-26; and it
reached its mid-point in the fall-winter 1942-43 when the
first sustained atomic reaction in Chicago was achieved,
signalling the beginning of the "Atomic Age". In 1863 Baha-
'u'llah publicly announced that he was the expected Divine

---

*The Peace of Ryswick between France and a Grand Alli-
ance of England, Spain and Holland marked the slow decrease
of French power and the beginning of Prussia's rise. The
Mexican expedition planned by the French emperor in 1861
marked also a loss of prestige by Napoleon III, which led to
the defeat of 1871 and the establishment of the German Empire.

Manifestation for the New Age -- with Saturn in Libra squaring Neptune; and the Bahai Movement began to grow and to promote an ideal, but very precise plan for a social and religious World-Order, the first religious movement ever to do so.

The cycle of Neptune appears to deal broadly (as already stated) with mankind's attempts to conceive and utilize an ever wider and more encompassing frame of reference for his institutions. Such attempts can ultimately succeed only to the extent to which an increasing number of human beings are able to feel compassion and to develop a mentality stressing inclusiveness and wholeness (or synthesis) instead of exclusiveness and the analytical, quantitative, rational intellect. The power to use the tremendous power locked in the atom, which was demonstrated as Neptune entered Libra (in a sense, the seventh phase of its cycle) could enable man to really build a global all-encompassing society and to transform the basic relationships between individuals and between group, substituting a feeling of abundance and spiritual plenitude for the ancient sense of scarcity and the bio-psychic fears which so far have dominated the mind of man; but this nuclear power plus the horrors of chemical warfare (and at a lesser level the poisoning of the Neptunian expanses of the atmosphere and the ocean) could also destroy all life on the earth.

The north node of Neptune is located now at about Leo $11^{o}20'$. Neptune moved back and forth around that point when the future of the League of Nations (a typical Neptunian project) was debated in the United States, and the Senate voted against ratification -- when President Wilson collapsed, and the Prohibition Act went into effect with demoralizing results. The woman suffrage amendment was also ratified. A couple of years before, the Bolshevik Revolution had changed the tide of world-history. World-Communism was also a Neptunian movement, as (especially in its first phase) it operated as a "religion of humanity", fanatic in its materialistic approach and its method.

An earlier passage of Neptune at its north node occurred during the years 1755-57, the time of the Seven Years War in Europe with its repercussion in America. It coincided with Franklin's first unsuccessful attempt at creating a union of the American colonies under a president appointed by the crown and a council of delegates elected by the colonial assemblies. This was the time when Free Masonry, the Encyclopedists and a number of pioneering scientists were stirring up the intellectual elite of the Western world and preparing the Revolutionary Movement which was soon to follow.

A still earlier passage of Neptune at its north node (15-92-93) coincided rather fittingly, even if negatively, with the dreadful Wars of Religion, and the gradual development of the American colonies. The transits of around 1426 came at the time of the revolt of Bohemia after the murder of John Hus, of the Hundred Years War and Joan of Arc (burnt in 1431). This period can be said to mark the first appearance of the concept of "nation", at that time a broader concept of social organization than those known during the feudal Ages. Two cycles before, we reach the era of the first Crusade which opened the mind of medieval Europe to the culture of the East.

Here, let me state again that a study of such planetary cycles should not focus on special dates marking their beginning and on precise correlations with historical events; it should rather study the entire pattern of the cycle in an attempt to discover the structuring forces at work underneath or within the historical events. What is important is the relation of any such event to the process as a whole which the cycle outlines and defines.

What matters today, for instance, is the fact that we are past the mid-point of the Neptunian zodiacal cycle which began in 1861 (Neptune entering Aries). Neptune in Scorpio is in the eighth phase of that cycle, and we are facing the im-

perative need to transform and regenerate what began at that
time -- mainly the results of the Industrial Revolution, of
colonization by Western powers, and -- let us be honest --
of our murderous attitude towards the American Indians and
of our miscarriage of the process of "emancipation" of Negro slaves.

THE CYCLE OF PLUTO

Pluto reached Aries 0° in February 1822 (heliocentric
position.) It had barely crossed the Aries threshold in geocentric longitude for a few weeks around the summer solstice 1821, at which time it was in exact square to a conjunction of Uranus and Neptune at the entrance of Capricorn.
This was also the year when Mars, Jupiter and Saturn were
conjunct in late Aries. Napoleon died in St. Helena on May
5th, 1821. An epoch was closing. Reactionary movements
dominated Europe; yet South American states were formed
through the liberating action of the great Bolivar and (in
Mexico) of Iturbe. 1821 witnessed also the start of the war
of Grecian Independence in which Lord Byron died. The new
bourgeoisie was rising to power. The Victorian Age was
imminent.

We have not yet come to the mid-point of this Pluto cycle. Pluto will reach Libra in September-October 1871; very
soon indeed. It could be a very important turning point, especially for the United States, as Pluto will be stationary at
what I stated already to be the Mid-Heaven of the U.S. "birth-
chart". There will be a Presidential Election in 1972, just
after Pluto crosses for the third time this Mid-Heaven. Neptune transited this point at the time of the first atomic nuclear reaction; Uranus, at the 1968 Elections (not yet witnessed as this is written); then Pluto at the 1972 Elections.
This must be highly significant. A new "America" may have
emerged by the mid-seventies; and in 1980 -- also an Election year -- Jupiter and Saturn meet also very close to this
same zodiacal place perhaps stabilizing the change in gov-

ernment, in fact if not in theory.

In December 1983 heliocentric Pluto will reach Scorpio and remain in that sign until September 1995. While passing through Scorpio the planet moves as fast as it ever does, indeed faster than Neptune. It reaches its perihelion (nearest point to the sun) in 1988, at Scorpio 12°43'. Just before entering that zodiacal sign Pluto cuts across the orbit of Neptune and finds itself closer to the Sun than Neptune. This is a most interesting phenomenon due to the great elongation of Pluto's orbit -- which in this resembles, on a much larger scale, that of Mercury. One could speak of it as a fecundation of Neptunian ideals by the relentless activity of Plutonian factors. The period was said to last nine years, according to the astronomer Hugh Rice (New York Planetarium); but more recent astronomical calculations estimate it to extend over twenty-two years -- between November 1978 and May 2000.

Pluto can be said, in one sense at least, to symbolize the seed falling into the humus made of the dissolved and chemicalized remains of the ending cycle of annual vegetation (the product of a Neptunian process of dissolution); it can be related also to the "Descent to Hell" by Christ before his resurrection. As Pluto therefore cuts into Neptune's orbit, a process of release from the past and of impregnation by a nucleated vision of the future can symbolically be said to occur. Indeed such a period in every revolution of Pluto around the sun is historically speaking unusually significant.

The last one occurred just before 1750 -- a time when ideas and men were born that were to dominate the revolutionary upheavals which followed some 30 years later. A Pluto cycle before brings us to the time of the Great Voyages, the "discovery" of America by Christopher Columbus, and the beginning of the Renaissance. Still earlier crossings of Pluto through Neptune's orbit bring us to the 1240 period (the struggle between Popes and Emperors, Mogol invasions, the destruction of the Albigenses and the entire culture of Southern France which had a great impact upon chivalry and the idealization of woman and love) -- to the great crisis of the year Thousand when, after the expected "end of the world" did not come, a new impetus was given to Europe leading to the great Gothic culture and the universalistic Medieval Order -- to the beginning of the Carolingian Kings in France after the great victory of Charles Martel over the Arabs which saved Christendom from Islam -- and eventually to the beginnings of the Christian era.

We are therefore coming to a period of great importance in the Eighties of this century -- less than twenty years ahead of us -- a period made even more significant by the heavy concentration of six planets in Capricorn in 1989 and 1990 -- particularly Uranus, Neptune and Saturn. Pluto in Scorpio will then find itself in constructive sextile to this group, and thus able to exert a tremendous power of reorganization and integration -- which could mean the beginning of a world-society, probably under a great personage.

Pluto was near its north node (Cancer $19\frac{1}{2}°$) when it was discovered. This coincided with the Great Depression of 1929-30, which led to the F. D. Roosevelt Administration and the New Deal which changed the whole spirit of America. If we take this crossing of the north node as the beginning of the Pluto cycle -- in terms of the unfoldment of Pluto's most typical characteristics -- we can easily see how significant this 1929-30 date is. It marks also the rise cf Mussolini and Hitler, the spread of the Communist ideology under Stalin, and the rapid development of our new technology. When Pluto reached its north node during the 1680's Louis XIV, and the Versailles Court with its pompous rituals, reigned. The Revocation of the Edict of Nantes (1685) marked an exodus of Protestants from France which parallels similar movements of population in Nazi Germany, Russia, etc. A previous crossing of the north node by Pluto leads us to the time of

Joan of Arc, the beginning of the national sense in Western Europe, and soon after to the fall of Constantinople by the Turks which brought also an exodus of scholars to Italy and led to the Renaissance.

Let me stress once more that what is essential is not the correlation of the start or culmination of a planetary cycle and some historical event, but the fact that these cycles enable us to understand more deeply the nature of historical processes and to ascertain more objectively our present place in the evolution of mankind. This applies as well to the study of the smaller and faster planets when related to the birth-chart and the life-span of individual persons (i. e. transits). But when we deal with the cyclic movements of the planets beyond Saturn we are no longer taking in consideration the development of individuals in themselves, but rather of individuals as participants in the larger rhythms of human society and of the evolution of the earth and the biosphere.

Today, as mankind is at long last compelled by its own inventions and its abstract intellectual development to think in terms of its global destiny and its all-human unity, this sense of participation in our entire planet's evolution -- and indeed of responsibility for what we now can do, for better or for worse, to this evolution -- must be developed by all significant human beings. The study of the cycles of the planets of our solar system can be a vital help to the growth of this impersonal historical and global realization in individuals ready and willing to assume the new role now open to mankind.

III. CYCLES OF RELATIONSHIP

Linking Uranus, Neptune and Pluto

In my book THE LUNATION CYCLE I have discussed at length the meaning of the distinction which should be established between "cycles of positions" and "cycles of relationship". The former deals with the successive positions of a moving object with reference to its starting point, and until the time of return to this starting point. Cycles of relationship, on the other hand, are cycles established by the successive conjunctions (and oppositions) of two moving celestial bodies.

A cycle of positions measures the course taken by any dynamic impulse from start to finish. It is as if a seed were watched becoming a full-grown plant, and the full-grown plant bringing forth again a seed while leaves and stem disintegrate -- and all this cyclic development occurring in vacuum without any outside interference or anything contributing to it. Obviously such a picture of growth in vacuum is a pure abstraction. It does not correspond to actual reality, because no impulse is left to develop without its course being modified by other factors. Life is based on relatedness; and so is civilization and every type of human activity. Even God's activity, I believe, would be meaningless unless it be understood in relation to the need of chaos -- that is, as an answer to the need of the materials left to disintegrate in space, remains or waste-products of a completed cycle of cosmic manifestation. God is absolute all-encompassing Harmony. "Compassion", wrote H. P. Blavatsky, "is the Law of laws". It is absolute Harmony in operation.

"Cycles of relationship" are best exemplified in the lunation cycle, from New Moon to New Moon; and whatever can be said of such a cycle can be said also, in general outline, of all such cycles -- for instance, of the often discussed 20-year cycle between successive conjunctions of Jupiter and Saturn. However, cycles of relationship are particularly significant when the two moving celestial bodies are of the same type, but of opposite polarities. This is the case with the Sun and the Moon in geocentric astrology, because the Sun and the Moon are considered merely as discs of light of equal sizes, the former having a permanent shape, the other being subject to constant changes; the Sun symbolizing the masculine and the Moon the feminine poles of being, Spirit in contrast with Life, etc. Likewise Jupiter and Saturn are two planets referring fundamentally to the social and religious life of man, and they act as polar opposites: Jupiter as an expansive, Saturn as a contracting force.

Jupiter unites men by making them expand and flow into each other through all means for social interchange, commerce, and religious communion. Saturn seeks to establish every man in his proper place in society -- that is, in his own frame of reference and individuality -- and to define all structures and boundaries. Thus the cycle of conjunction of Jupiter and Saturn reveals the periodical way in which the balance between these two polarities of communal living operate. The conjunction indicates a new start in relationship (new social adjustments and periods of reorientation), the opposition, a climactic moment at which whatever was begun at conjunction time either reaches fulfillment, or breaks down after a failure.

At a time when human society was conditioned by geo-

graphical and tribal structures, when it operated in a steady
state and in terms of well-defined, quasi-unchallengeable instincts or laws, the cycle of Jupiter and Saturn was a most
effective way of measuring the rhythm of such a society.
Their conjunctions occur on an average every 19,853 years
(practically 20 years) and a number of characteristic phenomena are connected with their recurrence. A few successive conjunctions take place in zodiacal signs of the same
element (fire, earth, air, water). As the element changes,
a "Great Mutation" is said to occur. These changes are not
always clearly marked, and thus differences of opinion among
astrologers prevail as to which conjunction is the most characteristic. However the chart erected for the "Great Mutation" of January 25, 1842 has proven quite significant an
indicator of world-events ever since, and it is supposed to
be effective until Jupiter and Saturn conjunctions occur in
air signs.

After 60 years, moreover, the two planets are found within a few degrees of their initial positions; and this 60-year
cycle was basic in the old type of mundane astrology. A larger cycle of 794.372 years encompassing forty Jupiter-Saturn
cycles has also been noted, in which the whole series of conjunctions in the various signs of the Zodiac is repeated, or
nearly so -- according to L. H. Weston. Other astrologers
claim that the complete larger cycle is one of 960 years.

Today, however, as humanity has left behind the relatively stable state of tribal-geographical organization and is
moving about in a state of reorientation toward a new condition of society based on universal all-inclusive values and
global wholeness (instead of the old state of tribal-national
exclusivism and so-called "sovereignty"), it seems quite
evident that the Jupiter-Saturn cyclic pattern can no longer
satisfactorily measure the historical periods. In a sense,
it was always more or less subservient to a larger all-human and global rhythm, but this rhythm could only operate
underneath the recorded events of history, unbeknown to the

men who made history.

In the preceding chapter, I discussed the respective cycles of Uranus, Neptune and Pluto; but I considered only "cycles of positions" (sidereal periods), and not the cycles formed by the successive conjunctions of these planets the one to the other. The interesting thing, however, is that because the periods of the three universalistic planets are very close to being in the simple ratio of 1, 2, 3, their mutual "cycles of relationship" produce a basic figure almost identical to those which have been mentioned. The most basic period, however, is one which approximates 500 years; and it seems that just as the rhythm of the conjunctions and oppositions of Jupiter and Saturn scans the melodic flow of history in so far as the destinies of smaller tribal and national communities are concerned, the rhythm of the cycle of relationship between Neptune and Pluto establishes the pattern of development in man's unceasing effort at emerging from the lesser to the greater social units. This effort is indeed the very substance of civilization as a process of universalization of values.

THE NEPTUNE-PLUTO CYCLES

This cycle, measured by the time elapsing between two successive conjunctions of the two planets, lasts close to 493 years. The geocentric conjunctions are usually repeated three times, so that it may be better to use the single heliocentric conjunctions as points of reference or milestones in the process of change. There were heliocentric conjunctions, according to available tables, in 1892 A.D.; 1399 A.D. around 906 A.D.; around 413 A.D.; around 81 B.C.; around 574 B.C. Every one of these dates refers to a crucial change in civilization, or in the striving of cultured peoples toward a universal civilization. It is possible also that the cycles of Uranus are closely interwoven with this Neptune-Pluto pattern; for in 1395-96 A.D. Uranus in early Sagittarius was opposing the Neptune-Pluto conjunction, while there seems to have been an at least from 577 to 574 approximate triple conjunction of Uranus, Neptune and Pluto near 580 B. C.

This period witnessed the reform of Gautama, the Buddha (according to the Hindu chronology), the birth of Pythagoras, the fall of Jerusalem; and indeed this sixth centruy B. C. began a completely new phase in the development of the human mind. In a lesser manner, the fifth century A. D. (which saw the final breakdown of the Roman Empire), the tenth century A. D. (which witnessed a new birth of culture, the Romanesque style) and the years around 1400 A. D. (which marked the spiritual beginnings of the Renaissance Movement) were also most important milestones in the vast evolutionary process which gradually is leading Man to a universal civilization.

I mentioned already the fact that, as a result of the great eccentricity of Pluto's orbit, this planet, when closest to the sun, moves faster than Neptune. This leads to a peculiar situation in terms of the aspects between the two planets. For over 90 years Neptune and Pluto remain in nearly the same angular relationship. Today these two planets form a sextile aspect. This aspect began, one might say, when Neptune reached Libra in 1942-43 while Pluto was located in early Leo. This sextile aspect will last until nearly 2030-2040; and it constitutes, as it were, the deep bass-note supporting the chord of faster shifting planetary relationships. As the sextile is a constructive and steadying aspect, this "long-sextile" of Neptune and Pluto constitutes a most hopeful factor in an otherwise tense celestial situation. It should mark the beginning of a new order -- perhaps of a global civilization and a true World-Federation.

During the eighteenth century -- from about 1698 to 1792 -- Neptune and Pluto formed a "long-trine" aspect. The trine is an aspect referring to expansion of consciousness or "vision" -- and this eighteenth century has been called the "century of lights". The light was only intellectual and rational, but it nevertheless led to the Revolutionary Era which saw the birth of political democracy and liberation from many old Medieval dogmas.

The preceding Pluto cycle saw also a "long-sextile" which corresponded to the Renaissance; so that we might hope on that basis that our present-day crisis will in some way be a "Renaissance". However all conjunctions of Neptune and Pluto, and the long-lasting aspect which follows, need not be considered constructive in terms of the then dominant culture. The conjunction of the beginning of the tenth century did mark the beginning of the great Catholic order of the Middle Ages, and of the Kiev Russia after Rurik the Great; but the conjunction of the fifth century in Taurus occurred as the Roman Empire was about completely to collapse. However, the break-down of the Roman Empire led under the sextile of Neptune to Pluto, to the rise of new kingdoms, particularly that of the Franks under Clovis, who, by becoming baptized in the new religion, began the cycle of North-European Christianity.

URANUS-NEPTUNE CYCLES

The cycles of relationship of Uranus and Neptune are very significant, because these two planets are in many ways complementary. Uranus is essentially the planet of individualism, referring to the hidden genius in every man and to its inspirational revelation. Neptune, on the contrary, is the symbol of collectivism and of the pressure of the collectivity upon the individual. The conjunction of the two planets occur at about 171-year intervals, and advance regularly, it seems, in the Zodiac.

Sepharial has a good deal to say on these conjunctions and refers particularly to the one which occurred in 1650, falling in Sagittarius 16th and 17th degrees, in exact opposition to the Ascendant of the city of London. This was the time of Cromwell's dictatorship, and on 1666 the famous great fire destroyed a vast portion of the city. It fell also on what may well be the Ascendant of the United States. Sepharial gives to the conjunction a rather destructive meaning: "disruption of old and effete institutions and laws, revision of codes and desposition of governments, new social methods through stress and insurrection", the latter timed particularly by the coming of Mars and Saturn to the places of conjunction or opposition to this Uranus-Neptune conjunction.

The period around 1650 marked indeed the very end of the medieval political system almost everywhere on earth; from Japan and India (where the Mogol dynasty began to crumble) to France, where the F r o n d e marked the last attempt by the nobility to oppose the absolute power of the king, Louis XIV, then dominated by Mazarin. The old Russia began to collapse and Peter the Great started (after 1689) to build modern Russia. Holland freed herself from Spain. And the American colonies after a series of upheavals, began to feel their growing power (New York became English August 27, 1664). During the 171-year period which followed 1650, the Classical Era of European culture reached its apex, crystallized rapidly and broke down during the Revolutionary and Napoleonic Era.

When Uranus and Neptune came again in conjunction in 1821, Napoleon I died, and the period of the Industrial Revolution and the era of railroads and of new labor-saving machines began. This was also the definite starting point of the Romantic movement. Liberals struggled in Europe against the despotic governments which followed Napoleon's debacle, and in South and Central America, new republics emerged from the domination of Spain and Portugal. In the United States, the Missouri Compromise (1820) marked the seed-beginning of the Civil War, and in 1823, the Monroe Doctrine established the ideal of Pan-Americanism.

The Uranus-Neptune conjunction of 1821 occurred in March in the third degree of Capricorn. Two more conjunctions (1993 and 2164) will also take place in Capricorn. In most cases, however, only two conjunctions seem to occur in one zodiacal sign. This could be taken to mean a special insistence on Capricorn -- a strong Saturnian zone. Political crystallizations are indeed especially powerful as humanity is seeking to fight rather senselessly against the inevitable organization of all its members into a global society. Uranus and Neptune stress the wider horizons of a world made "one world" by the discoveries of science and the tremendous increase in human interchanges. Three times their conjunctions are seeking to open up the fortified walls of nationalism, to eradicate the folly of power-politics in an electronic, atomic civilization and to inspire men who, like Capricornian President Wilson, seek to find ways of globally structuring the new world of mankind.

The third conjunction of 2163 falls a century after the time I have suggested for the beginning of the Aquarian Age; and at the very end of Capricorn. It will probably sound the final death-knell for the old world of European nationalism, seed of the Piscean Age. This does not mean that national cultures will not remain as organic entities within the larger global pattern. Nations or geographical regions in which people of the same language are gathered most likely will retain their relatively autonomous character as units of social management, but minus the separative political concept of "absolute sovereignty" -- the modern equivalent of the "divine rights of kings", against which men like Paine and Jefferson fought stubbornly.

We have just passed through a sextile of Uranus and Neptune which precedes the 1994 conjunction. This will no doubt be a very significant one, for it ends a series of other conjunctions in Capricorn, with six planets occupying repeatedly that sign for a couple of years. The period actually begins with a conjunction of Saturn, Uranus and Mars around the first degree of Capricorn in the spring 1988, then proceeds with a conjunction of Saturn and Neptune in 1989. In February 1990, Neptune, Uranus, Saturn, Mars, Venus and Mercury are in Capricorn opposed by Jupiter. We might well say that the sextile of Uranus and Neptune which precedes such a massing of planets can be seen as a warning, or even as a prelude to social and spiritual challenges -- and possibly telluric disturbances -- which are expectable.

It seems that these conjunctions of Uranus and Neptune provide us with a very valuable indication of the process by which larger ideas flow into the mind of Man. They indicate the time for the clearing away of Saturnian crystallizations. Then as the collective mentality of human beings becomes more open to the spiritual downflow, the "seeds" deposited into that collective mind at the time of the conjunction of Neptune and Pluto are able to produce a really new "vegetation" -- new institutions, new ways of life. The fact that the soon to come conjunction of Uranus and Neptune occurs at the time when Pluto is found "within the orbit of Neptune" (fecundating it, as it were) should be very significant.

I should add that most likely the two or three generations of great thinkers which p r e c e d e the conjunctions have a part to play quite different from those which f o l l o w it. The former are iconoclasts and pioneers (cf. for instance, the men of the Elizabethan Age like Francis Bacon, and those of the Revolutionary Period like Thomas Paine); while the latter are more like seers who envision new worlds and new human ideals (for instance, the scientists and mystics of the Classical Period, and the great humanitarians, socialists and religious leaders of the 1830 to 1850 period). We are now ready to witness, and are witnessing, the appearance of men whose task it is to challenge the old Christian-European culture -- first destroyers (in science and politics), then prophetic pioneers. By the time the century ends, a new influx of minds will come to bring us real visions of the new Aquarian world.

The number which characterizes the Uranus-Neptune cycle is significant, as 171 equals 9 times 19 -- and these two numbers, 19 and 9, are the "sacred numbers" of the Bahai Movement, whose new calendar (established by the Bab about a century ago) features a division of the year into 19 months (plus four holidays before the Spring Equinox) and a cycle of 19 years (roughly corresponding to a period of the Moon Nodes).

THE URANUS-PLUTO CYCLE

Because through 1965 and 1966 Uranus and Pluto were three times conjunct in the zodiacal sign, Virgo, this cycle takes on just now a very crucial meaning. Much of what is unfolding in the world as these pages are written some four years later can be related quite significantly to events which began a rather drastic process of social and ideological change, the ultimate consequences of which we can only guess at.

It is interesting to note that California (and also the city of Los Angeles) are technically "ruled" by Virgo. Because of this, there had been a strong expectation of telluric catastrophies, major earthquakes, etc. at the time of these Uranus-Pluto conjunctions. What happened actually, though less spectacular, may prove to be just as important. The revolt of students in the Berkeley campus of the University of California in 1964 was the spark that ignited a long series of similar events all over the world; and the Negro riots in Watts (the Los Angeles black "ghetto") also became a model for many such riots.

Uranus and Pluto were also in conjunction in 1850 - 51.* The Industrial Revolution was then beginning to change the

---

*The Uranus-Pluto cycle seems to be quite uneven. There was a conjunction in November, 1710, at about Virgo 2° -- a time filled with all kinds of wars, but which was to see soon the start in London of the great movement, Free Masonry (1717). The spring 1598 saw another one at about Aries 19°; this was the close of the Elizabethan Age, and the year of the famous Edict of Nantes which ended the wars of religion in France.

conditions of existence of entire classes of people. Even the colonial fever which led European nations to invade Africa and Asia brought white and colored races together. But this "bringing together" (i.e. conjunction) occurred in a spirit of conquest and greed, and under conditions of often extreme brutality -- which of course was bound to result eventually in violent revolt.

In 1850-51 Saturn was also in conjunction with Uranus and Pluto; but in 1965-66 Saturn was in opposition to the Uranus-Pluto conjunction. In 1850 the privileged classes, represented by Saturn, were able to use for their own aggrandizement the new powers generated by the Industrial Revolution. The conjunction occurred at the very end of the pioneering sign, Aries -- with Saturn bringing the energy generated by this Uranus-Pluto conjunction to the very first degree of Taurus, sign of productivity. The aristocrats and wealthy merchants of last century sought and achieved a vast increase in human productivity -- which in turn led to a proliferation of human beings. This time, Saturn in Pisces having opposed the conjunction of Uranus and Pluto in Virgo, humanity can no longer tolerate the possession of the resources and of the processes related to this conjunction by only a small minority -- not even by the white race, enjoying enormous abundance while the colored races in Asia, Africa and South America remain under-developed (in our sense of the word "development") and mostly under-nourished.

The Uranus-Pluto conjunction in the critical sign, Virgo -- which seems to refer so well to our college-bred intelligenzia, whether young or old -- is now confronting the Saturnian classes which hold still dominant power and constitute the now so sharply and vehemently criticized "Establishment". And this confrontation is taking a very drastic aspect, a thoroughly world-wide revolutionary aspect.

A conjunction of Uranus and Pluto is essentially a mindtransforming "influence". It refers to a situation which demands a very basic and thorough change of mind. Until 1930

Pluto of course was not publicly known to mankind. Its power was more related to the collective unconscious than to any conscious will to change. But now consciousness is focusing deeply compulsive drives through ideologies, opinions, slogans which can move the multitudes -- and modern media of communications involve the whole of humanity in such apparently insignificant events as a protest of college students in Berkeley or Columbia University.

Uranus and Pluto symbolize in a rather fascinating manner the atomic bombs or reactors using uranium or plutonium. They represent even more broadly our whole technologically-controlled society, our computerized business and (soon) education, our T. V. determined political Elections, In every field of human activity and individual responses, these technological procedures, and the mentality which both gave them birth and has been spreading everywhere as the result of this technology, have produced a radical transformation of human values and ways of life.

In Greek mythology Ouranos was the primordial power that rules over the vast expanses of space. Pluto, at a later phase of development, became the symbolic ruler of the depths of existence. In astrology today Uranus is the great power of transformation which has its beginning in a d e s c e n t of creative energy from spiritual heights of being; while Pluto is the power of the Underground and the generic Unconscious, the subterranean energy which brings all superficial constructs and all man-made institutions to the atomized condition of dust or humus, yet which performs this catabolic task as a prelude to a new kind of integration and potential rebirth.

A conjunction of Uranus and Pluto is therefore a kind of union of height and depth. Uranian creativity allied with Plutonian revolutionary disintegrative force becomes a ruthless and relentless force. Today it symbolizes the growing power of those elements in our society which have judged our technological and White-dominated society worthless, and condemned it to chaos -- a chaos believed to be a necessary condition for the emergence of a truly new mentality and society. This is what many of the rebellious youth in Paris, in May 1968, proclaimed; and indeed what so many people in our nation more or less vocally (and most often quite confusedly) claim -- whether they be student activists or Negroes intent on exercising by all possible means "Black Power". And the confrontation with the Saturnian Establishment and its police-force or army goes on, and may well grow far stronger and widespread, even if controlled for a while by the frightened mood of a still overwhelmingly large majority seeking to retain at any price their security, their gains and their suburban comfort; which means inevitably a kind of more or less overt military dictatorship or "Fascism".

The massing of seven planets in Virgo at the New Moon of August 23, 1968, plus the solar eclipse of September 22nd on the last degree of Virgo -- and other astrological indications of a more transitory nature -- add their very powerful testimony to those already mentioned. They suggest that large-scale events and crucial changes may well be in the making. Our twentieth century began under a near opposition of Uranus to Pluto. Indeed Neptune and Pluto, emerging from their 1891 conjunction, were pitted in Gemini against all other planets in Sagittarius; and the New Moon of December 2, 1899 had seven planets in this last zodiacal sign, with Jupiter just about to enter it.

We are living indeed in a "schizophrenic" century -- a "Civil War of Man"; and the opposition of Saturn to the conjunction of Uranus and Pluto has simply been bringing to the fore more vividly than ever the confrontation between two types of mentality, between the haves and the have-nots, between generations. Perhaps as Uranus and Pluto form again an opposition during the twenty-first century, the issue will be even more definitely settled, and what remains of the old world will give way before the rise of a New Age, the Aquarian Age.

In order to understand what is meant by such a new Age, we have now to study the vast cycle of the Precession of the Equinoxes, and to consider the rhythmic, cyclic processes which affect not only human civilization, but the entire planet, Earth -- and especially the earth's biosphere, within which all living beings are born, struggle for self-maintenance and self-expansion, and die, reabsorbed into the Plutonian physical and psychological humus which will once more be food for new generations.

PART TWO

IV. STARS, CONSTELLATIONS
AND SIGNS OF THE ZODIAC

There is perhaps no topic around which as much confusion and as many possibilities of interpretation have arisen as that referring to the cycle of the precession of the equinoxes and to the twelve "Ages" which constitute twelve sections of such a cycle. Even the exact length of the cycle is uncertain, as it probably varies; besides, two somewhat different cycles seem to be involved, one dealing with the motion of the equinoxes, and the other with the motion of the poles of the Earth. Above all, especially of recent date, a basic controversy has arisen concerning the very nature of the zodiac; and we are confronted today with two schools of astrological thinking, one favoring the t r o p i c a l zodiac, the other the s i d e r e a l zodiac. The tropical zodiac refers to the twelve SIGNS of the zodiac, the sidereal zodiac to the twelve CONSTELLATIONS. And to make the confusion worse, the signs and constellations bear the same name (Aries, Taurus, Gemini, etc.) though these names refer to two basically different entities and two even more different mental approaches to the concept of "zodiac", indeed to astrology as a whole -- and I should add, to essential human values.

In this chapter I shall not try to go into the many aspects of the controversy or to be too technical, even if this leads to some over-simplification. I shall attempt to explain the over-all situation in terms of what is the main purpose of this book, i.e. an elucidation of what is confronting mankind today -- an elucidation which seeks its supporting evidence from both the historical and the astrological fields. I am perfectly aware that in so doing I shall displease many people who will inevitably find fault with some of my statements and my interpretations.

Most of the data used in modern astrology are produced by calculating the positions of celestial objects with reference to two basic circles of motion: the earth's rotation in its equatorial plane, and the apparent yearly path of the sun, the ecliptic. The latter is interpreted today as referring to the orbit of the earth in its yearly revolution around the sun; while the plane of the earth's equator is made to extend infinitely in space, becoming thus the "celestial equator". The planes defined by the celestial equator and the orbital revolution of the earth do not coincide. They are inclined in relation to each other at an angle of approximately $23°5'$. Thus they cross one another; and the line of intersection between the celestial equator and the ecliptic define two opposite points which we call the spring and fall equinoxes. In terms of zodiacal longitude, these two points are said to represent respectively longitude $0°$ (Aries $0°$) and longitude $180°$ (Libra $0°$).

However, the relation between the two basic circles or planes of motion, equator and ecliptic, has been proven not to be fixed. First, the angle between the two planes is periodically changing, varying as it does within approximately $2\frac{1}{2}$ degrees limits -- such variations having a probable cycle of about 40,000 years. Secondly, if we consider the ecliptic fixed, we shall see that the equatorial circle has a twisting, sliding motion around it -- which results in a gradual displacement of the line of intersection between the two circles or planes. Actually the earth-orbit changes form gradually; but the variations in eccentricity, and in the position of the "line of apsides", determining the shape and direction of the orbit, are slow and of relatively small magnitude. They do affect, however, the cycle of precession of the equinoxes.

We are aware of the path of apparent yearly motion of the sun in the sky by observing the different stars which appear at the horizon, week after week, before sunrise and after sunset. In other words, we can plot the yearly path of the sun on the background of the "fixed" stars; thus giving it also a fixed character (if we ignore the very small motions of the individual stars in cosmic space). If therefore the line of intersection of equator and ecliptic very slowly changes place, it follows that when the sun reaches this line in its motion along the ecliptic, its position at the moments of the year called "equinoxes" also changes from year to year in relation to the fixed stars.

This fact is put in concentrated form by saying that the place of the equinoxes changes every year with reference to the fixed stars. The change is slow, a little over 50 seconds of arc a year, or one degree in less than 72 years. Thus, the equinoxes return to the same point of the ecliptic, and (theoretically at least) to the same star, after some 25,868 years have elapsed. This period, divided by 12, gives us the duration of any of the twelve precessional Ages. We are apparently now in the Piscean Age, and as the motion of the equinoxes is "retrograde" (i.e. in a direction opposite to that of the sun and the moon) the next Age will be the Aquarian Age.

CONSTELLATIONS VS. SIGNS

The stars which can be taken as indicators of this periodical displacement of the equinoxes are naturally those found near the ecliptic; and these stars -- indeed all stars -- have been grouped for millennia into "constellations". The names, sizes and boundaries of such constellations have differed in various civilizations; but some definite parallelisms can be established between variously defined constellations if one does not go too far in making the comparisons.

Evidently, either the tendency to group stars into constellations to which, more often than not, the names of animals
were given corresponds to a world-wide human desire. It
may very well be a projection of the concept of animal "tot-
ems" -- so basic in archaic tribal societies -- upon the celestial sphere. Even in Greek mythology we see human her-
oes or personages of special significance glorified into constellations in the sky -- somewhat as the Catholic Church
canonizes its saints and gives them "feast days" in the ritual
of the sacramental year.

The sky, for ancient societies, was the great symbol of
order and creative activity. Stars and planets were seen as
the bodies of gods. The sky as a whole represented the "world
of formation", the world of creative gods and hierarchies of
divine minds; and the whole concept of celestial constellation
has, I feel certain, a mythological origin. This does NOT
take anything away from its meaning, for myths are extremely potent factors in the evolution and formation of human
consciousness; and modern science itself contains a number
of myths, which now are referred to as premises, postulates, or perhaps "universal constants", the constancy and
universality of which -- I repeat -- is a matter of belief,
even if the values to which these "constants" refer are based
on proven facts -- but facts in o u r p r e s e n t e a r t h-e n-
v i r o n m e n t, which does not mean always and anywhere.

However this may be, the great problem concerning the
twelve zodiacal constellations -- groups of stars found on
either side of the ecliptic -- is the determination of their
boundaries. Not only have these boundaries presumably been
changed, time after time, but according to various occult
traditions, their number has not been always twelve. H. P.
Blavatsky claimed that originally there were only ten. Besides, several civilizations had "lunar zodiacs" divided into
27 or 28 "mansions" before they had "solar zodiacs". There
is no real reason to believe that our zodiacal constellations
should all be of equal size (i. e. covering each 30 degrees of
longitude) and when the International Astronomical Union in

1928 sought to remedy the uncertainty of boundaries by defining these by celestial circles, parallel and perpendicular to the celestial equator, the result was quite puzzling.

What we call zodiacal SIGN in astrology is something entirely different in principle from a constellation of stars. A zodiacal sign is simply one-twelfth of the ecliptic -- that is, a 30-degree section of the apparent yearly path of the sun (the earth's orbit in the modern heliocentric system). A zodiacal sign belongs to the t r o p i c a l zodiac, while the twelve zodiacal constellations belong to the s i d e r e a l zodiac. Both unfortunately bear the same names. The tropical zodiac is measured in terms of degrees of longitude, and it begins at the point where the sun crosses the celestial equatorial plane in a northward direction at the spring (or vernal) equinox.

At the spring equinox the sun has longitude 0°, and also declination 0° ("declination" measures the distance of any celestial body north or south of the celestial equator). This means that at the spring equinox the sun sets exactly at the west, that day and night are of equal length, and that the days are growing longer. At the fall equinox the sun has longitude 180° and also declination 0°, but then it is crossing the celestial equator in a southward direction. The days and nights are of equal length, but now the nights are growing longer.

As already said, the line of intersection of the ecliptic and the equatorial planes changes progressively because of a particular earth-motion -- a kind of wobbling motion somewhat similar to that of a top -- which alters the direction in which the polar axis is oriented. This polar axis as a result, points in the course of time to different "pole stars"; it describes a circle in space in about 25,000 years. At one time a star of the constellation Cygnus was the pole star (about 16,400 B.C.); at another time it was Wega (12,700 B.C.). At present, Polaris, in the constellation Ursa Minor, is our pole star, and the north pole will point to it more closely than ever next century. In due time, around 13,000 A.D., Wega will again become our pole star.

In describing the gyrating motion of the north pole, one has to speak of pole stars, because if we want to become clearly aware of this motion, it has to be referred to some relatively fixed point in the sky. The stars do move, but their motions are relatively so slow that for rough practical purposes we call them (unfortunately, I believe) "fixed stars". The planets, by contrast, move quite fast in the sky; so that primitive man, contemplating the night pageant of the sky, called them "wandering stars". It is for the same reason that in trying to establish and to measure the slow movements of the equinoxes it was necessary to refer the change to a seemingly "fixed" frame of reference.

This means that when the sun now is at longitude 0° (i. e. crossing the celestial equator from south to north, and sunsets begin then to move toward the north-west) it does not point to the same "fixed star" that it did at the time of the spring equinox two thousand years ago. For this reason we say that the sun is moving by retrograde motion from one star-group (i. e. constellation) to the next star-group. For instance, it is said (unfortunately) to enter, or to be near entering, the constellation Aquarius -- while what is "entering" this constellation is NOT the sun, but instead the vernal equinox-point. Because of this we are said to be at, or near, the beginning of the "Aquarian Age".

There was a time when the sun at the vernal equinox was pointing to the separation between the constellation Aries and the constellation Pisces; that is to say, at the spring equinox of that time, the earth, the sun and the boundaries between the constellations Aries and Pisces formed a straight line. When that happened, the SIGN Aries (the 30 degrees of longitude just after the spring equinox point) and the CONSTELLATION Aries coincided -- and the confusion between zodiacal signs and constellations of the zodiac did not exist. The problem is, however, to discover when this happened -- and it is a problem that CANNOT be solved on any astronomical or astrological basis alone, simply because we have

no way of knowing precisely w h e r e the boundaries between the constellation Pisces and Aries should be located.
This, simply, because such boundaries are man-made and
w e h a v e n o w a y o f k n o w i n g who established them,
when or for what purpose. One can talk forever about when
the Egyptian or Chaldean year started, what star they considered to be the most important one for this or that purpose,
when this or that astrological system of symbolism (like the
concept of "planetary exaltation") was adopted; but, however
fascinating a subject of enquiry this may be for archeologists
and ethnologists, this refers only to old traditions all involved
in mythological concepts, the key to the interpretation of
which are probably lost or not understood as the men of the
period saw their meaning.

I certainly do not wish to dispute here the findings of Cyril Fagan related in his book ZODIACS, OLD AND NEW (London, 1951), for I have not his competency regarding the Egyptian and Chaldean records. My point is simply that, even
if he were entirely correct in his deductions and interpretations of old tablets, all that this would show is that the Egyptians, Chaldeans, and Hindus apparently used a zodiac of
constellations in terms of a probably common tradition --
perhaps originating in the fabled Atlantis. Then during the
Greek period before Christ, something happened, and gradually a new conception of what the zodiac meant was intro-
duced, possibly by Hipparchus around 139 B.C. -- possibly
also as the result of the expansion of the Greek picture of the
universe following Alexander's conquests.

Mr. Fagan interprets this change as a terrible blunder;
but this interpretation may well be quite biased. It may more
accurately be the expression of a basic change of mentality
in mankind -- a change which marked this extraordinarily
important period from the sixth century B.C. to the first
century A.D. -- from Buddha to Christ; and I shall discuss
the meaning of this period in a subsequent chapter. It was
indeed a turning point in human evolution.

THE NATURE OF ASTROLOGY

Perhaps one of the basic issues, in this controversy between proponents of the two zodiacs, refers to the very nature of astrology; it involves also a general attitude to mankind's evolution. Most astrologers today have a tendency to think of astrology as a very special "science" which presents to us definite facts and direct causal relationships to the universe, discovered after long centuries of patient observations by generations of star-gazers. They see the zodiac as something as real and tangible as, let us say, the Van Allen bands which surround our globe. The ordinary astrologer likewise takes for granted the validity of an accumulated astrological "knowledge". For him, astrology is a thing apart, having its holy traditions; and, according to the siderealists, this tradition suffered a dreadful perversion -- somewhat as Catholics used to think of Luther's Reformation.

A variety of theories have been formulated to try to explain what actually the zodiac is, as a factual astronomical entity. The zodiac's division into twelve constellations, the shapes and the basic meanings of these star-groups (very heterogeneous ones, in many cases!) have been taken as if they were truths obtained by divine Revelation. Perhaps they are; no one can prove or disprove it. I simply do not follow such a line of thought, perhaps because I see astrology as the practical application of a basic universal philosophy which, while it is not at all new, nevertheless should be given a quite new, modern formulation so as to become a valid and convincing basis for a truly modern (or is it "future"?) human mentality.

I feel that astrology has always been -- when formulated as a system of thinking -- the application of a weltanschauung (world-view) the scope of which was much more extensive than the mere observation of the sky and the attempt to forecast coming events on this planet, Earth. This is why I said that the constellations of the zodiac are mythological entities; they are extraordinarily significant images, just as the Tarot cards or the Yi Ching hexagrams and their pictorializations are most significant symbolic pictures. All this zodiacal lore -- including rulerships and exaltations as well as the four elements, etc. -- are not the most essential factors in astrology; and certainly they should not be set once and for all as dogmas.

Astrology, as I see it, essentially is dealing with cycles of motions and cosmic (or bio-cosmic) rhythms. It is dealing with "form" or gestalt -- with structuring principles inherent in every organized system of activities; thus in every whole. It is not a question of literal, direct, external influence exerted by some celestial body upon entities living on this earth. Astrology is a way of studying and understanding the arrangement or organization of a few essential functions and drives in every organized whole of activity. In olden days this concept was expressed as the structural correspondence between microcosm and macrocosm; but originally it was the entire earth which was seen as the microcosm, analogical in basic structure to the whole universe. Only later on as the process of human individualization proceeded and individual persons emerged from the all-pervading and totally controlling collective matrices of tribal societies, did such individual persons come to be regarded as microcosms -- a fact which Jesus powerfully affirmed when he said: "The kingdom of heaven is within you."

This was a startling statement for men whose consciousness was still moulded by the basic experiences and beliefs of the tribal order; and in a very real sense it set astrology on a basically new foundation. This foundation was well understood in the Syria of the time of the Crusades. We find it developed in Medieval Alchemy, and stressed by the great Paracelsus, and in a somewhat different way by Boehme. Theirs was the true astrology -- not that of the kingly or princely courts of the Renaissance and the Classical era.

The astrology which built the zodiac of constellations and all that belongs to it refers fundamentally to what has been called the "Vitalistic Age". It was the Age that presumably saw the rise of agriculture on the banks of large rivers -- whether in China, Northern India, Mesopotamia or Egypt -- and the development everywhere of "cults of fertility" and "Solar Myths", later expanded in a variety of "Great Mysteries". An earlier period of human evolution refers to the Animistic Ages in which men saw everywhere "spirits" and sought to propitiate them; but Animism blended with Vitalism -- and it is still with us in a new form (the "atomistic approach" to the universe) -- while the Vitalistic imagery of the Mediterranean cultures before Christ was re-embodied under new names in the rituals and festivals of the Catholic Church. Traditional zodiacal astrology is largely influenced by such earlier approaches to existence.

To say that this zodiac of constellations is mythological is merely to say that it was a creation of a type of mentality which stressed greatly -- and for this period of history most validly -- the myth-making faculty of the human psyche. Our modern science has succeeded in bringing such a faculty in great disfavor; but recent psychological schools of thought and practice are once more emphasizing its value in psychotherapy. Many individuals today long for this mythical world to which they had become alien. And this is no doubt one of the reasons for the resurgence of interest in astrology, particularly among the young people who refuse to become identified with, and integrated in our technological and computerized social-political system. I am very much in favor of a new development of the myth-making faculty; but mankind needs new myths and a new feeling of relationship to the universe, and not the re-instatement of the Egyptian, Chaldean or Hindu imagery. We have to start afresh from the facts of our modern experience enlarged by the discoveries of modern astronomy. Astrology interprets the facts which astronomy and physics reveal to us -- but I mean here really facts and not merely hypotheses which change every few years.

I have no doubt that sooner or later a "galactic astrology" will develop as a result of our so-called "Space Age". In it man may transcend the limitations of our geocentric and narrowly heliocentric approach. It would describe the relationship of a human observer anywhere to the galaxy. Such an astrology would deal with stars, but not as "fixed" celestial bodies. It would see them as functional units in the immensely vast system of activities which we call the Milky Way. Such a galactic type of astrology would presumably use as a base line the intersection of the plane of the celestial equator (a prolongation of the actual equator of the earth) and the plane of our lentil-shaped galaxy (the Milky Way). The recent discoveries made by Dr. Giorgio Piccardi, director of the Institute of physical chemistry in Florence, Italy, concerning the effect of still unknown cosmic radiations on water, seem to link the observed effect with the constantly changing relationship between these two planes (cf. Michel Gauquelin's book COSMIC CLOCKS first published in French under the title "L'Astrologie devant la Science".)

Unfortunately we know so little as yet about the stars as individual sources of radiations, or as "cells" in the vast cosmic body of the galaxy, that it is very difficult to interpret their meaning, and the Medieval lore about the "fixed stars" is certainly not reliable. Nevertheless, when we deal with humanity as a whole -- as a functional system of activities within the earth-entity, we are confronted with the vast process of unfoldment of human civilization and it is to this process that the precessional cycle refers.

This cycle, I repeat, is one of the three most basic cyclic motions of our planet -- the other two being the day and the year cycles. The day refers to the sequence of stages or levels at which the consciousness of man operates; the year, to the series of yearly changes in the manner in which solar energies operate on our globe, stimulating cyclically the rhythm of life on the earth-surface. The precessional cyc-

le refers to the gradual, but basically periodical transformations of the collective consciousness of mankind -- and, we may assume, of other life-species.

I should add here that this precessional cycle, being
the result of a motion of our planet, refers essentially to the
unfoldment of what is inherent in the earth itself as an
organic whole. On the other hand, the cycles of the planets
which compose the solar system should be considered as
frames of reference for the effect of the solar system as a
whole upon the earth. The planets are external factors; they
refer to what happens in our immediate cosmic environment.
Their combined motions within the vast spaces which are
filled with radiation from the sun produce very complex currents, and everything on this earth is affected in some way
by these whirlpools of energy.

The stars also are centers of radiation within the larger
cosmic whole within which the sun and the entire solar system is revolving at immense speed. If they represent anything in the symbolic language of astrology, it is the presence of transcendental Powers -- powers to which we may
be related in various ways, constructive or destructive, when
we emerge from the womb of earth-bound consciousness and
rise beyond the compulsion of biological-emotional drives
which are inherent in the nature of the solar and lunar forces
animating our body and psyche. But I am speaking here of
single stars, or perhaps of groups of closely related stars
-- related by their age and the direction of their motions --
and NOT of man-made zodiacal constellations along the path
of the apparent annual motion of the sun, the ecliptic. Single stars are actual facts within the Milky Way; constellations
are mythological images. The two must not be confused.

STARS ARE NOT "FIXED"

The stars are not fixed; they all have their proper motions. If they do not appear to move appreciably even during a thousand years, it is because they are so far away

from us. We consider the zodiac of constellations as the
"fixed zodiac" simply because we take it as our frame of reference -- i. e. as a fixed background upon which we can project, plot and measure the motions of the sun, the moon and
the planets. But why not reverse the procedure and say that
it is the equinoxes that are the fixed base-line and that it is
the stars which move in relation to it in a 26,000 year period, called by some authors, the Great Sidereal Year? Actually astronomers operate in this manner, except that they
measure the positions of the stars mainly in Right Ascension
(i. e. with reference to the celestial equatorial plane) instead
of in celestial longitude (i. e. with reference to the ecliptic).

Nothing is motion-less in the universe; and all motions
should be related to the observer. This is astrological "relativity" -- a definitely modern concept. Man is the observer; and normally his basic post of observation is his birth-
place. The universe is as he sees it. The stars move in one
day around his earth-location; they move through ideally defined twelve sections of space, above and below his horizon
-- and these sections are what the astrological Houses should
be, but which in fact our zodiac-haunted astrology forbids
them to be. These same stars move also during the Great
Year across the ecliptic; that is, their celestial longitudes
change from 0° (the beginning of the s i g n, Aries) to 360°.

These are the f a c t s relative to the human observer;
and astrology should be today "person-centered" rather than
geocentric. It deals with the relationship between a single
individual person and the whole universe of which that person
is the centèr. He is truly the center of the universe b e-
c a u s e h e o b s e r v e s i t c o n s c i o u s l y. Everyman, if
he be truly a microcosm, is the center of his own universe.
At least this must be so in "natal astrology". If we deal with
global Man spread all around the globe, then a "geocentric"
astrology is required. Everything changes according to the
point of view, because each point of view produces its own
frame of reference for measurements. Each man faces the

world from his own individual station -- or else he is only a non-differentiated unit in the collective whole constituted by his tribe, his culture, or today, his nation.

The whole world confronts the individual person at every moment. The one purpose of astrology is to help him to understand the meaning of this ever-renewed confrontation. If he understands well this meaning he can offer a valid, significant and therefore "creative" r e s p o n s e to the universe. And that is the only thing that counts in human life: to be able to give at every moment a creative, thus significantly transforming response to whatever greater Whole within which the individual person is operating -- whether it be his community, his nation, humanity or the whole universe.

In order to be able to give consciously and definitely such a response, a man must realize what he really is as a person born at a certain time of human history and at a certain place within a society structured by a traditional culture -- or trying to break away from such a culture and allowing a new one to arise. Moreover, a human being extends not only in space, but also in time. The individual person is not only what he is now, but the entire series of now's from birth to death. Man is not born an individual person. He becomes one in concrete fact from day to day. He is constantly in process of actualization. And it is this process -- which is the true meaning of the word "destiny" -- that astrology can help the individual person to understand. The Great Sidereal Year cycle can also, to some extent at least, help us also to understand the place which, collectively today as mankind, we are occupying -- the phase of the process of mind development (which we call "civilization") through which our generation is now living and struggling.

It is the coming of the great stars to certain critical points within our basic frame of reference, the ecliptic, that may tell us the story. That is to say, if a particular brilliant star reaches longitude $0°$ it will find itself, symbolically speaking, fecundating with its radiations the spring season of the year. It will be in conjunction with the sun at the vernal equinox. If it has longitude 120° it will be conjunct the Sun when the latter enters the zodiacal sign, Leo.

There was a time -- around 3000 B.C. -- when according to the old Persian astrologers, "four Royal Stars" were pointing to the four directions of space, marked by the equinoxes and solstices. Aldebaran (constellation Taurus) was pointing to the East, pouring its radiations then upon the springs of our northern hemisphere. Regulus (constellation Leo) was pointing to the South, and the summer solstice. Antares (constellation Scorpio) was pointing to the West, and the fall equinox. Fomalhaut (constellation Pisces Australis) was pointing to the North, and the winter solstice.

Today Aldebaran is located in the zodiacal s i g n Gemini (about 9°); Antares, at about 9° Sagittarius; Fomalhaut, at about 3° Pisces; and Regulus at the very end of Leo -- entering what I called the Sphynx degrees (Leo 30th degree and Virgo 1st degree), because the Sphynx, being half-lion and half-Virgin, obviously represents symbolically the transition between Leo and Virgo. Regulus was entering the s i g n Leo in 137 B.C. (according to the astronomer Hugh Rice), i.e. it had longitude 120°; and this may be another way of defining the beginning of the so-called "Piscean" Age. Regulus will reach longitude 150 degrees (the sign Virgo) around 2010 A.D. The great star Betelgeuze in the constellation Orion, will enter next century the sign Cancer (longitude 90°) -- thus it will pour its energies upon the summers of our northern hemisphere; and this will be one of the factors pin-pointing the beginning of the so-called "Aquarian Age", as we shall see later on.

It is the position of the stars as well as of the planets and other astrological factors with relation to the equinoxes and solstices which should essentially be considered as the most significant indicators of what is taking place in the evolution of mankind; just as the positions of the sun, moon, planets (and, at least in some cases, of the stars) in relation to the actual horizon and the zenith-nadir vertical axis of the birth-chart are the most significant factors in defining the particular individuality and destiny of a human being. The planets' places in the zodiacal signs (i.e. their longitudes) and the aspects they make to each other refer more to the specific character of the energies of the person's nature; that is, to the particular kind of human being he is.

It is evident that the attitude which I have presented in the foregoing is diametrically opposite to the one prevalent in astrology. The astrologer speaks of the retrograde motion of the equinoxes during the precessional cycle -- or even worse, of the successive entrance of the Sun in Pisces, Aquarius, Capricorn, etc., as if the Sun were "entering" anything at all! This is -- I repeat -- because for traditional and even contemporary astrology, the zodiac of constellations is the fixed frame of reference. I am saying instead that it is the stars that move in relation to the tropical zodiac of signs; and they move in the normal way, constantly increasing in longitude.

Thus if we can at all say that we have passed through most of the Piscean Age, it is because the stars gathered under the mythological figure of the two Fishes have been coming to the spring equinox, radiating their light upon our vernal beginnings -- i.e. "influencing" (symbolically speaking) the way man in our Northern hemisphere has met the challenge of being an originator, a pioneer, an "Aries type" (Aries being the name of the first zodiacal sign of spring). As we reach the so-called Aquarian Age, it will be the stars grouped by tradition under the constellation Aquarius which will be conjunct with the Sun at and after the vernal equinox.

The whole picture is actually exceedingly. simple. All you have to do in order to realize its significance is to forget astrological textbooks and students of past cultures, and open your eyes to the rhythmic phenomena which tell us of our relationship, as beings constituting living cells in the vast body of the earth, to the regularly moving dots and discs of light in the sky. We can supplement these observations today with the knowledge given by our sense-extensions -- telescopes of various kinds, spectroscopes, radars, etc. -- but we do not need to pay much attention to old traditions and the mythical imagery devised by obsolete cultures of the past. We should create new images, for we are indeed at the threshold of a new era.

If we are to go to the past for some clues which may help us to free ourselves from recent traditions, let us go to a very ancient past. If we did, we would see that most likely the first way in which men sought to measure the rhythm of the seasons was by studying the cyclic displacement of the location of sunsets at the western horizon. Only at the equinoxes does the Sun set exactly in the west, and rise in the east. At the winter solstice the Sun sets some 23 degrees farther to the south; at the summer solstice, to the north. This solar motion is measured in astronomy in terms of degress of declination. It is related to the phenomena of the seasons because it refers to changes in the angle at which the Sun-rays strike the earth-surface throughout the year. It produces the increase and decrease of days and nights. And in my book THE PULSE OF LIFE I discussed this yearly cycle as a constantly changing relationship between two forces, the Day-force and the Night-force, which correspond to the well-known Chinese dualism of Yang and Yin.

This approach to the cycle of the year is, I believe, more basic than that which uses the apparent passage of the Sun through zodiacal signs or constellations. It is at least more primordial. It provides us inescapably and graphically with four basic points in the year's cycle: the solstices and the equinoxes. It is the foundation of the very old esoteric concept of dividing the year into two halves: one during which "the Sun moves northward" -- related to the spiritual development of the individual, according to the occult tradition -- and the other during which the Sun moves southward, which refers to the growth of c o l l e c t i v e values.

It seems evident that the great stones of Stonehenge in England, and similar ones in Central America, served largely as markers determining the phases of this yearly movement (in declination) of the Sun. But they also presumably were able to pin-point the position of some brilliant stars at certain times, not only of the solar year, but also of the Great Sidereal Year of 26,000 years. At least it is quite certain that the Egyptian Great Pyramid had certain of its narrow passage-ways oriented so that the rays of a particular star would strike the central chamber of the Pyramid. Esoteric tradition -- it is now widely known -- considers that the Great Pyramid was not, originally at least, a tomb built for some ambitious pharaoh, but the place of spiritual-occult Initiation. It claims also that it was erected a w h o l e c y c l e o f p r e c e s s i o n e a r l i e r than modern Egyptologists are willing to admit. The book of Davison, THE GREAT PYRAMID, is very well known and has been much quoted, attacked and defended. An archaeologist, Dr. Getzinger, whom I personally knew many years ago, showed me enlarged photographs of the side of the Great Pyramid which he claimed definitely revealed the incrustation of sea-shells at a certain level quite above the present level of the base of the structure. He believed that the Pyramid had been built indeed over 30,000 years ago by men of a very advanced civilization -- "advanced" perhaps not in terms of our materialistic technology which can only think of releasing power by d e s t r o y i n g matter (whether it be coal, oil or uranium atoms), but through the use of a very different kind of power centered in man himself. At any rate, it is interesting perhaps to note that Davison's date for the beginning of the new Aquarian Age was 1844 A. D., which differs by some five centuries from the date presented by Cyril Fagan who also studied Egyptian records, and from the dates accepted by one or the other of the schools of Hindu astrology.

And so I end this chapter on a note of uncertainty. This uncertainty is quite characteristic of the astrological situation as a whole; and it assuredly does not justify the claim made by so many astrologers today that astrology is a "science", in the precise modern sense of the term. It is based on scientifically obtained astronomical facts, we might well say; but astrology gives to these facts a human meaning and value. Astronomy does not -- except by its implied belittling of man as a small creature on a small planet in a not important solar system of our Milky Way, which is but one of countless galaxies separated from each other by incredibly vast distances. The answer by an astronomer to such implications was that nevertheless man is the astronomer who has been able to measure these enormous distances and cycles.

It is man's response to the events, the pressures, the infinitely complex facts he has uncovered which counts. It is not the greatness or vastness of what man faces, relative to his size and life-span, which matters; it is man's attitude toward these near-infinities. It is what his consciousness, facing them, makes out of them -- what he allows them to make of himself. And it is at that level that astrology can significantly operate; not at the level of the prediction of events which in themselves have no meaning, except the meaning which we give them. Events do not happen to us; we happen to events.

V. FROM BUDDHA TO CHRIST
The Great Turning Point in Human Evolution

It is well to re-state at this point the main purpose of this book. Humanity is evidently in a period of world-wide crisis brought about -- if one looks at the chain of social, political, economic and cultural-religious events during the last two to five centuries -- by the development of a new type of mind in the Western world. The development of an experimental, analytical and rigorously exact type of intellectual thinking led, under the special circumstances of European culture during the Renaissance, to tremendous advances in technology. These in turn altered the ways of life of Western man, the relationship between social classes, the conditions of labor, the life of the family, the cultural and religious beliefs of any country in which the white man came to exert a dominant and transforming influence. Today the whole of mankind has been caught up into this whirlpool of intense, accelerating change. The Electronic Revolution and the use of nuclear energy, the fast accumulating effect of ever-spreading industry upon the air, water and soil of our planet, and the psychological as well as social consequences of modern medicine, of automation and of globe-encircling means of communication have brought us to a relatively imminent point of crisis -- a crisis which could have the most radical and perhaps catastrophic effect on human evolution.

The question of questions today is: Whither mankind?

Two basic possibilities come at once to the mind. We may be facing an accelerated e vo lu ti o n which will lead to a more technological and more computerized and automated global society. This would take place probably under some kind of centralized control made necessary by the fantastic complexity of the problem of organizing group-relationships and economic-social management all over a globe swarming with billions of human beings with enormously varied cultural backgrounds, languages and dogmatic beliefs. On the other hand, it may be that we are at the threshold of a worldwide r e vo lu ti o n, the first aim of which is to make our present-day institutions and ways of life so un-operative that a state of global chaos is produced, in the hope that out of that chaos a totally new and better civilization will emerge. There are perhaps today no other alternatives, even if these two possibilities may well take forms very different from those which are most commonly imagined.

From this it should be clear that if astrological cycles have any validity at all at the level of mankind as a whole, they certainly should show that we are NOW in a period of crucial transition. Astrologers speak of the New Age, the Aquarian Age. Obviously if we are at, or close to the beginning of this new Age, our present world-wide crisis should coincide more or less accurately with the beginning of this Age. If there is no such coincidence, this means either (1) that our present world-crisis is not as important as we think (no more than, say, the revolutionary period before and after 1789), or (2) that it will become more critical during perhaps the next two or three centuries -- or else (3) that the precessional Ages do not refer to such critical changes in human society and in human consciousness. (This could mean that other astrological cycles are the ones which are the true indicators of world-wide human upheavals).

The hypothesis numbered (1) does not seem valid, insofar as, to man's knowledge, never has the w h o l e of mankind been involved in a radical struggle which could mean a nearly total extinction of the human race -- and never has the change in the most fundamental approach to society, religion, man, God, the universe been as all-encompassing and as deliberate, as bound to transform the lives of all human beings. Hypothesis No. 2 may be correct, but if so, the prospect it reveals is quite forbidding, and the hopes of many groups of people for a far more constructive and spiritual New Age beginning at some fairly close date are indeed tragically meaningless. The third hypothesis may also be a valid one, and it could be that other cosmic cycles than the Great Sidereal Year are now beginning, precipitating as it were ahead of time the crucial events normally expectable at the beginning of a precessional Age, thus making the transition between two basic phases of human evolution a long drawn-out one.

In this connection, I should refer to the 500-year long cycle of Neptune-Pluto conjunctions discussed in the preceding chapter, and to the 10,000 year cycle mentioned in the chapter before the last. There may be still larger cycles related to changes in the shape of the earth's orbit, or to certain phases within the (presumably) 200 million years long cycle of the Sun's revolution around the galaxy which might tend to accelerate evolutionary processes in all that lives or thinks within our entire solar system -- or any such solar system.

However, as already stated, each precessional Age (i.e. each "month" in the Great Sidereal Year of some 25,868 years) can be said to last roughly 2160 years. That is to say, the stars advance about 50 minutes of celestial longitude every year, or (in round numbers) 1 degree in 72 years. Now, if we can show that every 2160 years a very important crisis of transformation occurs, affecting at least the vanguard of human evolution, then this would give much validity to the concept that the succession of the Ages is indeed a significant indicator c l o c k i n g, as it were, the processes of history, at least at a specific level of change. If we can show that the internal pattern of these Ages (definable in as-

trological terms) corresponds significantly to the s t r u c-
t u r a l u n f o l d m e n t of the particular phase in human evolution that began at, or very near, the starting point of the
Ages, this correspondence would tend to prove the worth of
using such cosmic clock t o p i n p o i n t f a i r l y a c c u r-
a t e l y t h e p o s i t i o n o f m a n k i n d t o d a y. If we know
where we are at in terms of a long-term human evolution in
consciousness and in the capacity to establish steady forms
of social-cultural organization, we have reached a point of
vantage from which we can evaluate o b j e c t i v e l y -- and
no longer in terms of our personal or collective fears or
hopes -- the meaning of our present world-crisis. The purpose of this book is, I repeat again, to gain such an objective
perspective on our world-situation. It certainly is not born
of the desire to collate old astrological material and to provide some more data for the student of astrology to memor-
ize and to repeat for the edification of friends or pupils.

THE BEGINNING OF THE PISCEAN AGE

Various dates have been advanced on various grounds for
the beginning of the present "Piscean Age". The earliest is,
I believe, that given by David Davison in THE GREAT PYR-
AMID: ITS DIVINE MESSAGE. The date is 317 B. C. -- and
the Piscean Age is made to end in 1844 A. D. ; a span of 2162
years. In the ENCYCLOPEDIA OF ASTROLOGY by Nicho-
las de Vore (New York 1947) several articles written by
Charles A. Jayne -- who for several years published the remarkable magazine IN SEARCH -- give numerous astronomical data referring to the precession of the equinoxes (cf.
especially page 307-309), data which are rarely, if ever,
mentioned by astrologers.

One of these data deal with the "Invariable Plane" of the
solar system; another, very revealing, to the difference between the cycle of the gyration of the earth's poles and the
cycle of the precession of the equinoxes. This difference is
due to various factors too technical to mention in this volume,

but which apparently lead to rather important variations in the precise length of the precessional cycle -- from 25,413 to 25,976 years. The 25,868 year period, which was given by H. P. Blavatsky in THE SECRET DOCTRINE as well as in other books during the nineteenth century, refers seemingly to the length of the present precessional cycle. However, Charles Jayne states that the cycle of the poles last 25,694.8 years. He claims that a new polar cycle started around 25 to 28 A. D.

Gerald Massey, a deep student of Hebraic and Egyptian culture, gave 255 B. C. as the date for the beginning of the so-called Piscean Age. The astrologer Thierens gave 125 B. C.; Paul Council 0 A. D.; Cyril Fagan -- father of the Siderealist movement in present-day astrology -- 213 A. D. According to Gavin Arthur, the date should be 496 A. D., a date apparently given by Max Heindel and corresponding to the time of the baptism of Clovis, king of the Franks after defeating the Romans at the battle of Soissons in 486 -- events that marked the spread of Christianity in Germanic-French Europe. Celtic Ireland had been converted to Christianity some fifty years before; and Rome had been largely destroyed by Alaric in 410 A. D.

The fifth century A. D. date seems quite impossible to accept as the date when our sidereal zodiac of constellations and the tropical zodiac (of signs) coincided; but it points to something significant at the historical level -- that is to say, to the final collapse of the Roman Empire. Actually the Empire in the West could hardly be said to have existed as a real power after the middle of the fifth century. The history of ancient Rome lasted about one thousand years; and these thousand years witnessed most radical changes in the mind of Man and in the concept of social organization, in Asia as well as in Europe.

According to H. P. Blavatsky, "the close of the Archaic Ages occurred in 608 B. C." (cf. SECRET DOCTRINE). It is not clear on what that date is based, but it is interesting to note that 2500 years later Baha'u'llah -- who is regarded by the great number of Bahais all over the world as the Divine Manifestation ushering the New Age -- died in May 1892, thus just after the last conjunction of Neptune and Pluto. H. P. Blavatsky had died on May 8, 1891, and the year 1898 marked the end of the first 5000 years of the Kali Yuga according to the traditions of India -- an important turning point in the great 10,000 year cycle which has been already discussed in a preceding chapter.

The sixth century B.C. was undoubtedly a most significant turning point in human civilization. Gautama the Buddha was then living and bringing to mankind a new mentality. (Some traditions make him born in 563 B.C. -- others state that he died in 543 B.C. at the age of 80). It was the time of Pythagoras and Solon in Greece, that of Lao Tze and Confucius in China, and of the historical Zoroaster in Persia. The Babylonian captivity of the Hebrews began in 586 B.C. The old Egypt ended its long history and became a Persian province.

Five hundred years later, Rome became the dominant power in the Mediterranean world after destroying Carthage and annexing Alexandria, center of the late Hellenistic culture; and after another five centuries it collapsed as an empty shell kept in existence by its Army and the effectual administrators of its provinces. The glorification of this Roman civilization which has been traditional in European and American circles of learning has been a rather extraordinary phenomenon. It has been due no doubt to the fact that our Western culture has inherited from the Rome of the Caesars one of its basic Images or myths (in the deepest sense of the term) -- the other being the Image of Christ, the Redeemer and Savior of souls.

The Image of Caesar is that of a centralized form of social-political organization backed by a powerful military and administrative structure able to control an immense mass of slaves. We call this today "Fascism", in the broadest sense of the term. Against this Caesar Image stands that of Christ. The Administrative Order of Rome was confronted by the Mystical Order of Christianity, and the latter won. But having won and destroyed from within the Roman society, Papal Christianity re-embodied much of the ideal of "world administration" characterizing the Roman Empire in the partly-spiritual and partly-political patterns of the Catholic Medieval Order. The relative greatness of the Gothic culture of a religiously unified Europe has often been belittled by our modern civilization founded, in the early days of the Renaissance, upon a denunciation and downgrading of the Middle Ages. What concerns us here, however, is the chronological pattern of the development of our Western civilization; but in order to select the really crucial dates beginning the basic phases of such a development, we have to understand the nature of the forces operating underneath the superficial conflicts between States and personalities.

To reach such an understanding, we must go beyond Caesar and Christ in the past, and try to grasp the evolutionary meaning of the mental revolution which began with the great Sages and leaders of thought of the sixth century B.C. Beyond Jesus the Christ stands Gautama, the Buddha. The challenge of Jesus to the Administrative Order of Rome is rooted in the challenge of Gautama to the Caste-system of India -- and, beyond what had crystallized as a binding Caste-system, to the entire way of life, and the collective mode of thinking-feeling which characterized the Vitalistic era of human society.

This Vitalistic era was based on the principle of the multiplication of seed -- whether it be the vegetable, the animal or the human seed. "Increase and multiply" is the great command of the gods of tribal societies, agricultural and hypnotized by fertility and the dualism of sex. And the Catholic Church even now finds it still almost impossible to give up its subservience to this ancient vitalistic mentality conditioned by the principle of scarcity and the "struggle for life"

-- perhaps with a certain kind of prophetic (bio)logic, considering that we might be facing a world-wide catastrophy of one kind or another. On the other hand, what Buddha and Christ brought to mankind was -- stated in two different ways to fit two different types of racial-cultural mentalities -- the vision of a humanity freed from earth-bondage and from the classifications required for the proper functioning of a large-scale Administrative Order; freed also from vitalistic urges, sexual compulsions, and the drive for man-made comfort and sense-intoxicating abundance.

Buddha taught the conquest of Nature and of the vital forces driving man to an ever-repeated round of desire, frustration, pain and more desire -- a conquest through mental processes of unrelenting awareness. Jesus' method was that of total surrender to the will of God through the intensification of the basic feelings of love, trust and faith. The Hindu Krishna -- a great statesman -- had also taught a complete surrender of the human will to the Divine Will; but his teachings were focused apparently on a c t i o n. Buddha stressed the transformation of the m i n d, and Jesus that of the f e e l i n g s, the most powerful of these being "love".

According to the Hindu chronology -- which, of course, Western Orientalists do not accept, basing themselves probably on false or superficial concepts -- 25 centuries separate Krishna from Buddha, and 25 centuries more bring us to the turn of this century, the key-note of which someday may be seen to be "activism". And we find today a great Hindu personage, Sri Aurobindo, stressing the need for a total transformation of human nature, even at the level of the physical body -- i.e. the transfiguration of matter, and (at a collective all-human level) of society as a whole. But Sri Aurobindo, in a sense, combines the mental approach of Gautama the Buddha and the feeling approach of Jesus, as a foundation for the total transformation to be achieved through a synthesis of all the principal types of yoga -- devotional, mental and actional. It was in the Bhagavat Gita -- the teachings of Krishna to his disciple Arjuna on the battlefield where the fate of India was to be decided -- that Sri Aurobindo found his central inspiration; and his influence is now spreading widely from the Pondicherry ashram where he lived for over 40 years, and, sooner or later, from the new nearby city, Auroville, in which a community of 50,000 persons devoted to the building of a future humanity is expected to live and work.

The great thinkers, prophets and illumined sages of the sixth century B.C. began to build the foundation -- i.e. to sow the seed -- for a new humanity by breaking down man's attachment to local conditions (geographical and tribal-racial-cultural). They were the prophets of a universalistic order of existence -- beyond boundaries and social-political categories. But they could only address themselves to "individuals", to men able, ready and willing to take a crucial step of self-liberation and self-actualization as individuals -- individuals grouping themselves, in many instances, in monastic communities on the fringe of the prevalent social order, or (as we would say today) of the "Establishment". Buddhist monasteries and wider communities were formed in Asia; Pythagoras started his famous and ill-fated community of disciples in Krotona, in a Greek colony of Southern Italy.

Whatever the forms this sixth century B.C. evolutionary movement took outwardly, the basic fact is that it began a definite new "mutation" in the planetary Mind of humanity-as-a-whole. It built up, we might say, in seed this one Mind of planetary Man. Alas, negative trends operated soon everywhere. In India, Buddhism dried up into a kind of spiritual selfishness -- a seeking for "liberation" in complete isolation from the rest of mankind -- or became perverted because the lower castes had flocked to its ranks. In Greece, an extreme individualism bordering on anarchy and intellectualism for its own sake emptied the new mind of its real significance. The Greek states fought each other into subservience to Macedonian totalitarianism and to the emerging power of Rome.

Rome was needed to unite the crumbling Mediterranean cultures into a vast heterogeneous empire, which brought to a material and administrative focus the spiritual ideal of the great Sages of the sixth century B.C. It was, alas, a way of integration vitiated in its very foundations by an extraordinary sense of cultural-social pride and by the wholesale enslavement of conquered people. There was, of course, nothing new in slavery; but, necessary as slave-labor was for Rome's expansion and for its Administrative Order, it became nevertheless the cancer that was to kill from within the Roman empire.

The Christian faith and its apostles were not the only factors that destroyed Roman society from within; for a great variety of cults from the Near-East spread through the empire and in the ranks of the Army, all bringing to the Romans some more or less intoxicating yearning for a world-transcendence of the most un-Roman kind. And Rome finally crumbled under the attacks of the people from the North who had been "contained" for some centuries by the great military machine of Rome. Yet Rome had brought to humanity some basic social concepts which altogether fit into the complex realization of a world-wide Administrative Order -- using the term "world-wide" as it relates to the concept of "world" at any particular historical time. Today, both the Russian and the American schemes of social-economic-political organization embrace potentially the entire earth, and even the moon; this is our present "world". Science-fiction writers picture a "Galactic Federation"; that too would represent "the world", a world to be administered by a central Authority because of its immense complexity and diversity.

The concepts of "citizenship", of "person" (in a legal sense), or provincial adminstration, were really creations of the Roman mind. When they had been used before, it was with quite a different meaning -- even in Greece. To these legalistic concepts deeply inbued with the Roman drive for administrative efficiency and the Roman pride -- the pride of a "ruling race", to which the Anglo-Saxon culture has become heir -- Christianity brought a spiritual dimension. Christ's idea that every man is a son of God, that Heaven (the formative power which makes of every person a microcosm of the whole universe) is within each human being, that the one ultimate and all-transforming "law" in the Law of universal Love, parallels at the level of the spirit the basic Roman concepts, even though these ideals of Christ are opposed to the exterior manifestations of the world of Caesar.

In a very real sense, the Christian spiritual individualism n e e d e d the Roman concepts as earthly, concrete, social bases of operation. Jesus asked his disciples NOT to fight the Establishment symbolized by the Caesar-Image. He asked them to be "separate"; to go after his Father's business, to follow him even to the ultimate end, the Cross. The Hebrew world in which he had been born was divided in his time between the partisans of violent action and the upholders of what today we call "passive resistance" and "love-force" (or flower-power with the hippies -- these early Christians without Christ). How strangely modern this situation! Does it not suggest that the two epochs, in some sense, are parallel?

This has been, of course, Arnold Toynbee's contention in his monumental STUDY OF HISTORY. The difficulty is a matter of exact t i m i n g. Does the crisis our modern world is facing, in Europe as well as America, somehow parallel that of the closing centuries of the Greco-Latin civilization? Has the new "Christianity" already come, in a not as yet too well-known form (the Bahai Faith perhaps?), and are we already at the "bread and circus" phase of the Roman Empire or just before a truly global Empire? Are already Washington and Moscow, the two West and East polarities of our modern technocratized world, facing the two billions of underfed and under-developed human beings kept at bay by our atomic bombs? Or are such attempts at synchronism and historical analogies most misleading?

It is here that astrology can come in and state that there is a 2160-year cycle, and that it should be able to give at least a tentative answer to our problem. The reason it must remain tentative and somewhat inconclusive is that, I repeat, there is the possibility that the confluence of several cycles, small and very large, beginning at or close to our time, may precipitate certain processes. The interaction of the Neptune-Pluto cycles of some 493 years and the equinoctial cycle of 25,868 years may have accelerated, since 1892 (the Neptune-Pluto conjunction) the pace of events during the transition period between the so-called Piscean and Aquarian Ages. Above all, there is the possibility -- to me, a strong probability -- that the time at which the sidereal and tropical zodiacs coincided marked the beginning not only of one of the twelve precessional Ages but the beginning of a complete cycle of 25,868 years, a new Great Sidereal Year. If this is so, the meaning of the cyclic picture changes a great deal, for the events of 2000 years ago -- and of this century and the next -- are seen in a much broader perspective.

THE BROADER PERSPECTIVE

Of course our historical knowledge is so limited and so unreliable when the distant past is concerned that it is not easy to think in terms of cyclic units each lasting nearly 26,000 years. However, it is very interesting to note that, only a few years ago, it was estimated that the well-known cave-paintings discovered in Central France, Spain, Africa were made about 25,000 B.C. Prehistoric dating is always subject to change, but it is quite conceivable that these remarkable indications of a developed culture ("primitive" though we may consider it to be) occurred at the close of a precessional Age lasting roughly from 52,000 to 26,000 B.C. -- or perhaps during the early stages of the cycle which found its late culmination in the historical period of Egypt -- the

Great Pyramid being perhaps the remains of a more distant Atlantean-Egyptian civilization around 30,000 B.C.

There is no way, of course, to prove "scientifically" the validity of such dates or the existence of great civilizations on land now submerged by the oceans. I can only present as a hypothesis the idea that the first century B.C. marked the beginning of an entire precessional cycle of 26,000 years, and that what I have called elsewhere "the Christ-impulse" (cf. my book FIRE OUT OF THE STONE: A Reformulation of the Basic Images of the Christian Tradition, 1952-1962) is to be considered as the fundamental evolutionary drive characterizing this new cycle (i.e. from 100 B.C. to around 25,700 A.D.).

It seems to me that a new phase in man's evolution began which is based essentially on the eventual realization by every human being of his individuality as a single and unique person -- as a microcosm -- as a potential "son of God". The transcendental Sages of the Upanishad period in India and even Gautama the Buddha did not consider the individual person as a microcosm, but rather as a more or less illusory formation, the consciousness of which was deeply involved in the illusion of separateness; and the goal of the spiritual life was presented as a re-absorption of this temporary form of consciousness darkened by "ignorance" in the one infinite Reality, Brahman. Our Christian Western culture, on the other hand, has extolled theoretically and idealistically the "worth and dignity of the individual person", even if in practice it did very little to apply its ideal to social living. This ideal should now become a practical and social reality -- and of course this is the grand and glorious ideal of democracy. But this word, democracy, can hide a multitude of sins of omission as well as of commission. And we are facing the possibility that the coming decades will witness a complete betrayal of this ideal in this country which had most seriously tried to make of it a practical way of life.

If my hypothesis is correct, the basic "mutation" at the level of the human mind, of philosophy and religion, in the sixth century B.C. should be considered as a mutation within the "seed"-period of the last precessional Age ending about 100 B.C. Symbolically speaking Buddha is the seed; Christ, the germ. Germination is a crucifixion of the seed stirred by the power of sun-rays as spring begins. As this process of germination occurs, the nucleus of the seed sends a tiny rootlet down into the soil in order to assimilate the chemicals contained in the humus (the disintegrated remains of the vegetation that was); then a small germ which somehow manages to break through the crust of the top-soil and into the sun-light.

The upreaching germ is not the only product of the "crucifixion" of the seed. There is also the "rootlet"; that which feeds the new growth by reorganizing materials of the past into assimilatable food-stuff. There must be the Administrative Order; and the archetypal Image of that Order has been in the now ending Piscean Age, Caesar. Caesar polarizes Christ, as the root polarizes the flowering stem. But this may not be an inevitable kind of polarization. The Caesar Image may only belong to this ending 2160-year long Age which talked about Christ, yearned for, prayed to, perhaps suffered for Christ -- but was not able to build a Christocentric society.

We should not be astonished by this fact IF we realize that the Christ-Impulse and the ideal it carries is the original "Logos" of a cycle of 26,000 years; if therefore we are at the end of only the first of twelve sub-cycles. If the whole process is only beginning, how could we expect it to reach already a condition of perfect manifestation of its original Impulse and archetypal Ideal!

When we think of the Great Sidereal Year as a whole and of its twelve successive phases or periods of unfoldment, what we call mythologically the Piscean Age is seen simply as Phase One of a vast planetary and human process of evolution. This Phase One began around 100 B.C.; and Phase Two will begin around the mid-point of next century. Phase Three, some 2160 years later, etc. Looking at the matter in this way, we realize that it is confusing to speak of the "Piscean Age", because in astrology we usually think of Pisces as the end of a cycle -- whereas in this vaster context this Piscean Age is the beginning of the Great Sidereal Year! Of course the mythologically inclined astrologer will speak of the symbol of the Fishes in early Christianity -- but the great rival of Christianity, the religion of Mithras, which was so widespread during the Roman Empire, particularly among the soldiers, stressed instead the blood of the Bull, and Christ was also symbolized as the sacrificial Lamb; so that we find all these zodiacal symbols mixed up in the early centuries of the Christian era. One must be very careful when using symbols; and one should be sure that one does not select as "proof" of one's concept what justifies the latter, and forget the rest.

When the Piscean Age is understood to be the Phase One of the Great Sidereal Year, the meaning of the whole picture held usually in the astrologer's mind is indeed changed. The Phase One of any cycle can be said to resemble the weather in early spring, or the psyche of people born just after new moon; it is a highly subjective and often confused stage of growth during which the consciousness tends to be obsessed by great ideals and potentialities which it cannot yet objectively realize. The backward pull of the past is then nearly as strong as the drawing power of the future. It is a period of conflicts; and Jesus saw this well when he told his disciples that he did not come to bring peace, but a sword; that he came to bring fire down upon the earth; that, wherever he appeared, conflicts would arise between the members of any family, between fathers and sons. Christ is the Germ -- the tender, uncertain, insecure sprouting plant reaching to the light; and the first phase of the Great Year over which Christ will rule (from within the individual person) has brought forth only individual successes, and wholesale social failures, wars and tragedies.

What we speak of as the Aquarian Age will be the Phase Two of the cycle; and the number Two always refers to the substantiation of an originating Impulse or Ideal. Even the symbol of Aquarius -- the Man carrying an Urn from which flow celestial Waters -- should tell us that what will be at stake in this coming Age is the release of cosmic energies upon the Earth under the control of humanity. The symbol explicitly states that these energies have first to be captured, then condensed in some sort of container (or engine) from which they can be released downward to make fruitful the soil upon which we stand. I would therefore think that the keynote of the coming Age should be management; but what is at stake is perhaps not the management of the kind of forces Western man has released through the destruction of material substances (including atoms), but rather the controlled use of powers of a spiritual order which somehow man carries within himself. Man will take the responsibility for the release of such powers and for the results they will produce -- something that our intellectualistic scientists refuse to do.

A 100 B.C. STARTING POINT?

We must now return to the difficult task of trying to establish a significant date for the beginning of the Great Sidereal Year and of its Phase One, the Piscean Age. From what has been said about the Christ-Impulse it might be expected that the new cycle should start at the time of Jesus' life. But there is also a never quite ended controversy as to exactly when Jesus was born -- and even about who he was and what he actually did. Then there is the disturbing fact that the phrase, "the beginning of a cycle", is always ambiguous. When does a human being begin? At the moment of the impregnation of the ovum by the sperm, or at the time of the first breath?

When we study the present period stretching from the 18th to the 21st centuries it will perhaps become clear that what I once called the "Avataric Period" should be said to last three or even four centuries. A cycle begins successively at different levels. The Christ Impulse may not have to be linked only with the life of the man, Jesus. It may have operated before him. When does the germinating process begin? Certainly not when we can observe the small germ breaking through the earth-crust into the light of the day.

Jesus may indeed represent the Son-aspect of the divine creative descent of new power -- the actual embodiment of a new quality of existence, the prototype and exemplar. But before this concretization of the Christ-Impulse into a human person, there should indeed be an essential creative stirring up at the level of the planetary Mind; and this may be the Father-aspect -- and the Father, of whom Jesus constantly spoke, may have had some kind of "hidden" manifestation, perhaps a century or more before the appearance of the Son among men -- an idea which explains much concerning what is taking place today in our world.

We know that the Essenes referred in their recently discovered records to a great "Teacher of Righteousness" who must have lived before 100 B.C. There is also a Hebrew and Gnostic tradition studied by R. S. T. Mead according to which Jesus was born in 144 B.C. As I stated before, the star Regulus apparently entered the sign Leo (i.e. reached longitude 120°) around 137 B.C., and the astronomer Hipparchus who made a complete map of the heavens and of the zodiacal constellations lived at this very same time. I have felt for a long time that this star was the celestial "Guiding Spirit" of this Phase One of the Great Tropical Year. The name "Lion of Judah" may have some significance in this connection, as Regulus (the "little king") is the star supposed to mark the heart of the celestial Lion.

It was around 100 B. C. that the Mahayana School of Buddhism developed, stressing the ideal of the Boddhisattvas who renounce Nirvana and perfect bliss out of boundless compassion for all living creatures -- thus the primacy of "Love" over any other factor in man. Indeed the insistence on the universalizing power of Love (a g a p e) can be considered as one of the main key-notes of this Phase One of the Great Sidereal Year, for the basic drive of this entire cycle of 26,000 years is UNIVERSALIZATION -- while the key-note of the preceding cycle was most likely CULTIVATION (whether at the level of agriculture and cattle raising, or at that of human "culture" -- thus of the control of vital urges and of the sublimation of instincts through rituals and art-creations).

The drive for universalization operated in the Rome of Caesar and his successors at the root-level of the Administrative Order; without such an efficient group of administrators and a deep sense of "law and order" there can be no universal society. With Jesus, this drive had a transcendental and idealistic nature. And the dynamic and restless character of the Christian-European (and now American) cycle is an expression of this drive for universalistic knowledge -- for the conquest of what is always "beyond" the conquered and the experienced, for universally valid "laws", and for some single theory or formula which can be universally applied to solve all basic problems.

I believe that such a universalistic approach began to operate in the minds of men constituting the vanguard of humanity during the first century B.C., even though the thoughts of the great Sages of the sixth century B. C. prepared the way for such an operation. Exact dates in such matters are not very significant; yet we shall see in the next chapter how if one begins around 100 B.C. and one divides the 2160 year-long Piscean Age that follows that date in various ways consonant with astrological practice (decanates, degrees, midpoint of cycle) one sees clearly emerging a pattern of development which fits well the facts and elucidates the meaning of turning points in the historical process.

If we divide the 2160 period into its three "decanates" (a zodiacal sign of 30 degrees is said to include three decanates of 10-degrees each) we obtain three 720 year sub-periods; and if we begin the Piscean Age at 96 B.C. the first of these sub-periods ends at the very birth of Islam (the Hegira 623 A.D.), and the second in 1343. This was the time of the Hundred Years War between France and England which led to Joan of Arc and the birth of the concept of "nation", unknown until then. The Black Plague was ravaging Europe; the Gothic Era was ending, and a spiritual (or occult) movement of rebirth was beginning, which we can associate in Europe with the real Rosicrucian Movement and in Asia with the reform of Tibetan Buddhism by Tzong-Kha-Pa, Humanism was the next stage -- the Great Voyages which encircled the globe and led the entrance of the Americas on the planetary stage, the beginning of modern science and the Renaissance.

These two dates, or the middle of the seventh and the fourteenth centuries, divide the whole historical process of our (Piscean) Western-Christian civilization into three most significant periods. During the first, we witness the confrontation between the old Roman way of life and the Christian way, between the two great Images, Caesar and Christ. During the second period, the confrontation is between Christianity and Islam, a confrontation which dominates the whole Middle Age culture in Europe, which leads to the Crusades and all that these produced, directly and indirectly. The third period witnesses the third basic confrontation of this Piscean Age pitting Humanism and the spirit of modern Science against a Christianity rent in two by the Reformation (which was in itself an expression of nascent individualism and rationalism).

It seems to me that no other date for the beginning of the Piscean Age would offer such a clear-cut and absolutely fundamental division of the historical process, at least in so far as Christendom and European civilization are concerned.

However, it is obvious that personal opinions can greatly differ concerning what are the most significant turning points in the history of a civilization. Except for a man of synthesizing vision like Arnold Toynbee, modern historians (and even more all our college text-books) are myopically searching for small details and records relating the superficial facts of the everyday social or personal life. What is needed in order to grasp the rhythmic process of civilization and of the planet's evolution is the capacity to envision the whole process of human unfoldment in its successive phases. It is to develop what I have named an "eonic" consciousness, attuned to the vast rhythms of the earth, of the continents, of humanity-as-a-whole. This is the "holistic" approach to existence; and the main value of astrology, when properly understood and used, is that it becomes a specialized technique for the development of man's holistic mind.

VI. THE STRUCTURE OF THE
PISCEAN AGE

The division of a whole cycle into twelve phases seems to be as basic as the division of a circumference into twelve equal arcs of thirty degrees. To the Greek philosopher the whole universe appeared as a dodecahedron inscribed within a sphere. The number 12 is divisible into 4 and 3, and these numbers have always been given an archetypal and magical significance. Four is the number symbolizing concrete existence; the cube or perfect stone is the foundation of material life in most ancient mythologies. In astrology, the cross of horizon and meridian establishes the basic structure of the birth-chart. There are four seasons, four points of the compass, etc. Three refers to the realm of Ideas, or archetypes; and almost every culture has thought of the Divine under three aspects. In logic, or in the dialectic process of transformation of all existential wholes, one studies the sequence of thesis, antithesis and synthesis.

In the preceding pages, I spoke of the significant way in which the Phase One of the present Great Sidereal Year -- to which I shall still refer as the Piscean Age for convenience's sake -- can be divided into three periods of about 720 years. The first period witnesses the confrontation of the new spirit of Christ-Love with the administrative order of the Caesars; the second period refers to the crucial challenges to Christendom posed by a conquering new religion, Islam, and by the Arabic and Mogol peoples -- a profoundly significant challenge, if we consider the unitarian character of the Islamic Faith and its origins, and also the somewhat more obscure historical meaning of the expansion of Mogols and Turks living in what geopoliticians have called the "heartland" of the earth. The third period is filled with the progressive development of the modern spirit of humanism, intellectualism and individualism which produced modern science and our technological and materialistic society. This is the confrontation which is now disintegrating the very foundations of our Christian civilization. Whether a new and transformed Christianity will emerge as the inspiration of the coming Aquarian Age, or a totally new spiritual Impulse will play this role, this indeed is perhaps the most basic question-mark of our present time. The answer should be forthcoming within the next decades; and it may have been given -- but such an answer may not be evident until late next century, just as it certainly was not evident in the first or second century A.D. that Christianity would dominate the culture of Europe for two millennia.

If now, instead of dividing the 2160 years of the Piscean Age into three periods, we are using a binary system of measurement, we will see at once that the years marking the end of the tenth century A.D. become the dividing line. This, of course, is also most significant because it is during this tenth century that we find at work the forces which built the great Images which developed during the Gothic period of the Universal Catholic Order, and which indeed are still basic in our Western culture. It is for this reason that Oswald Spengler (in his famous book THE DECLINE OF THE WEST) considered the tenth century as the beginning of the European culture proper. The Romanesque style began to unfold, and the myths and folklore of centuries to come took form before the great crisis of the year 1000, when the end of the world was expected. When the world did not end, a feverish phase of expansion began in Europe, which apparently was paralleled by similar movements on other continents (cf. LES METAMORPHOSES DE L'HUMANITE, Editions PLANETE, 1965).

The first half of a cycle can always be considered the "descent into matter" of the regenerative spiritual Impulse which was released at the beginning of the cycle. The second half refers to the "ascent of consciousness" through significant forms. These forms are first what Spengler called the Prime Symbols of a culture-whole, then characteristic institutions and specific art-forms and language-patterns. To me there is little doubt that the end of the tenth century A. D. (around 983) stands out as the basic turning between what could also be called the involutionary and the evolutionary phases of the Piscean cycle.

If we divide the two halves of the Piscean cycle into two we obtain such dates as 443 A. D. which marks practically the end of the Roman Empire, and the march of Germanic peoples over the new lands they were to occupy; also the middle of the sixteenth century -- the Elizabethean Age, the Reformation, the Renaissance. The mid-fifth century is the turning point within the "involutionary" phase of the Piscean cycle (the conquest of space by the new "materials"); the mid-sixteenth century is the turning point in the evolution of European culture.

THE TWELVE-FOLD PATTERN

A closer analysis of the structure of the Piscean Age can be made by dividing it into twelve sub-periods of about 180 years. This, I believe, was attempted for the first time by Manly P. Hall, but instead of correlating these sub-periods with the twelve zodiacal signs, it seems more significant to relate them to the sequence of the twelve Houses of a chart, because the Houses refer to the series of basic experiences and tests through which an individual passes in the process of actualizing the potentialities inherent in his nature at birth.

Beginning thus with the year 100-99 B. C., we obtain the

following series of sub-periods. Let me again repeat that the dates marking the start of such sub-periods are only approximate, as the basic 72-year period (i. e. one degree of precession) is not exact, and there have been also changes in calendar and two ways of going from B. C. to A. D. dates (I use the historian's usual way).

I. 100-99 B. C. to 82 A. D.

The two fundamental Images of the Piscean Age are established: Caesar and Christ -- the State and its Administrative Order backed by military power, and the great Symbol of Redeeming Love, God become man to save humanity. In India, we have the similar figure of the Boddhisattva dominating the new Buddhism (Mahayana). As we come to the last period of the Age (1883-2060) we see, on one hand, the "Big business-military complex" (or the Communist Party leadership in Soviet countries), and on the other, a still inchoate group of movements devoted in principle to a spiritual or idealistic form of democracy and personalism -- with the rebellious youth of our day as the new Christians, as yet without Christ. Any "last" period of a cycle must solve the problem posited by the "first". The way any man dies is the solution (positive or negative as the case may be) to the life-problem his birth posited.

II. 82 to 262 A. D.

This period witnesses first the general reaction to the impulse started in the first phase of the cycle -- then the slow substantiation and growth of those products derived from that impulse. Christianity develops and the Pax Romana proves itself under Trojan.

III. 262 to 442 A. D.

The Christian impulse is being disseminated; ideological arguments and political conflicts develop. Neither the Roman Empire, nor the Christianity of the Gospels survive; but the "surroundings" (third House) are permeated with the concepts of both.

IV. 442 to 622 A. D.

This is a period in which new races are moving around in space in order to find the geographical lands which "belong" somehow to them; i.e. their respective "homes". Great confusion everywhere. Every group seeks to take root -- including the Church (Gregory the Great, 600 A. D.).

V. 622 to 802 A. D.

This period begins with the prodigious growth of Islam, westward, northward and also eastward. The Normans and Magyars invasions are partially checked. A very masculine period of bursting forth.

VI. 802 to 982 A. D.

Charlemagne is crowned by the Pope Emperor of the West; but his empire is divided at his death, establishing the future pattern of much of European history. Later on, Otto the Great is proclaimed head of the Holy Roman Empire centered in Germany -- and the imperial Image henceforth haunts many rulers, including Napoleon I (who felt he was a reincarnation of Charlemagne) and Hitler. The end of the tenth century witnesses some degree of political stabilization everywhere: in China, after years of anarchy, the Song dynasty begins in 960; the New Mayan Empire in 987, the year of the start of the strong Capetian dynasty in France.

VII. 982 to 1162 A. D.

The Crusades begin in 1096. In this "seventh House phase" of the Piscean Age, East and West begin to interpenetrate again. French noblemen are in the lead and establish various feudal kingdoms in and around Syria. As they return to France, they bring back with them the seeds of the "spiritual Renascence" of the XIVth and XVth centuries which preceded the "intellectual Renaissance" of the XVIth century. These French noblemen not only take Eastern wives, but mingle with mystic brotherhoods (Sufis, Druses and other groups) -- for which they are condemned by the Pope. Then are formed the great Knightly Orders, such as the Knights Templars (founded in 1119 A. D. by Hugues de Payns and

Godeffroi de St. Omer), the knights of the Order of the Hospital of St. John of Jerusalem (with Raymond du Puy as their most famous leader, 1120 A.D.), and later the Teutonic Order (whose origin dates from 1128, when a German pilgrim and his wife started a hospital on the shores of Palestine).

VIII. 1162 to 1342 A.D.

German, English and French kings lead Crusades against the Turks who, under the great Kurd ruler, Saladin, had reconquered several Islamic countries and Jerusalem. These Crusades (from the third to the seventh) ended with the abandonment of the Holy Land by the Christians (1291) and the eastward spread of the Turks (Mamelukes) who finally conquered Constantinople in 1453 -- thus ending the Eastern Empire begun under Constantine the Great (330 A.D.) During this strange and tumultuous period, the greatest beauty and fervor blend with the shadows of a feudal and theocratic society. It is the time of the Gothic cathedrals and of chivalry, but also of the ruthless suppression of spiritual-occult groups such as the Albigenses (who were heirs, in South-West France, to a great Gnostic tradition) and the Templars (who knew too much and had become spoiled by wealth -- wealth the French king badly needed!). It saw the rise of the Universities, and the works of great encyclopedical minds such as Roger Bacon, St. Thomas Aquinas, Dante and many Christian mystics, Alchemists and astrologers -- and of equally brilliant thinkers in Syria and the Near East, and also India. But it saw also the beginnings of the Inquisition around 1220 -- just at the time of the English Magna Charta and of the Swiss Confederacy, first steps toward "democracy". During these two centuries powerful political leaders arose, from Frederic Barbarossa to the great Mogol Khans, and the struggle between the Papacy and the Germanic Emperor was pursued relentlessly. The growth of mercantile cities in Germany (Hanseatic League, etc.) and Italy established the foundations for the eventual development of bourgeoisie and world-wide trade.

To interpret this Gothic period in terms of the different levels of eighth-House symbolism is to gain a new insight into its essential character. That "medievalism" is still today synonymous with fanaticism and ignorance merely indicates how deep is our bondage to the concepts of the Renaissance -- and it is not a too fortunate bondage! The Age of Scholasticism and of Chivalry is obviously not to be taken as an ideal model for the future society; yet, in its universalism and its insistence upon spiritual values, in its youthful enthusiasm for coherent learning and for creative group-expression, in its heroic venturesomeness and its bold artistic conceptions, the Middle Ages period, from 1000 to 1250, stands out as an extraordinary and fascinating epoch. It is indeed truly a seventh and eighth period within the span of the Piscean Age because its keynote is the transformation of human relationships and of society on the basis of a spiritual and universalistic (encyclopedical) vision. And nothing characterizes this keynote better than the spirit of chivalry.

IX. 1342 to 1522 A. D.

As we reach the mid-point of the fourteenth century and the third of the "decanate" periods of the Piscean Age, (which is also the ninth "house-subdivision" period) we see the human mind reach a new stage of growth and expansion. Historians often consider the date of the fall of Constantinople (1453), or that of the so-called "discovery" of America (1492) as the beginning of "modern history", but these fifteenth century events were foreshadowed by the long period of conflicts and of mental-social arousal which is contemporary to the Hundred Year War between France and England. No cycle starts on a strikingly positive note -- but only with a promise. Spiritually, the new tone sounds forth; but, materially and socially, what is revealed is potentiality and not yet concrete actuality.

The ninth House period of the Piscean Age begins thus with the Black Plague and the spread of sexual diseases, and with the Hundred Years War. It begins with the Golden Bull which establishes the pattern of the Holy Roman Empire and of the Electorate responsible for the perpetuation of the Empire -- and ends with the Diet at Worms which sets the prenatal pattern for the Europe of modern nations. It begins with the gradual breakdown of Scholasticism and the growth of rationalism, from William of Occam (1340) onward. And as Byzantine scholars flee from the impending fall of Constantinople, they bring to the West a much expanded knowledge of Greek philosophy and science. With the formation of the new Academy in Florence under the influence of Plethon (1356-1450) we can trace the birth of Humanism and the renascence of Platonism. It will take another century for the movement to reach its full development with men like Erasmus and Copernicus. The invention of the printing press around 1450 gives a powerful stimulation to learning at the very time the scholars from Constantinople are rushing to Italy, where the artistic Renaissance is being initiated under the patronage of men like the Medici.

This period, 1342-1522, begins the era of the great martyrs who die at the hands of the Inquisition and whose sacrifices give added vitality to the forces of building the new society and the new thinking -- from Joan of Arc, the first prophet of spiritual individualism and nationalism, to the Bohemian, John Hus, whose followers were among the first to use effectively gunpowder and crude cannons in their desperate struggle against the powers of Church and Empire lined up at the Council of Constance (1415). It also sees the beginning of the great adventures across the seas: the discovery of the Canary Islands and Azores around 1350, and a century later the search for new routes to India and the lands of silk and spices -- a search inspired by commercial purposes, after the fall of Constantinople had made impracticable some of the best overland routes to Asia. Columbus and Magellan, Cabot and Vespucci, Ponce de Leon and Cortez are the best known names of the period centering around

1500.

The three great inventions which made this European expansion at all levels possible (compass, printing and gunpowder) most likely came from China. In a sense, modern history and the spread of Western civilization was conditioned by them. The use of gunpowder rendered the medieval armies of noblemen obsolete, and gradually gave power to the bourgeoisie and the common people. It enabled a few Conquistadores to subjugate older and effete civilizations. The compass made world-navigation feasible. Printing provided the material foundation for the intellectual development of Europe. And the Reformation (1517), by applying the new spirit of individualism to religion, helped to transform the Catholic universalism of the Middle Ages into the nationalism characteristic of modern European history.

What develops through any "ninth House phase" always becomes consolidated and socially effective in the tenth House. Likewise the spiritual ferment which has been slowly activated during the fifteenth century produces strikingly objective and concrete social and intellectual results after 1510. Everything then happens at once: the effective conquest of the New World, the Reformation and the wars of Religion, the crystallization of the new type of social unit, the European nation -- above all in France and England under new ruling houses (Bourbon and Tudor) -- and the tremendous growth of the Renaissance spirit, in philosophy, literature, art and science.

X. 1522 to 1702 A. D.

This "tenth House" period can be divided into two phases. In the first -- 1523 to 1613 -- we see the occult-mystical tradition of the Gothic Age coming to its fruition in great Alchemists, Fire-Philosophers and Rosicrucians. The Rosicrucian Brotherhood was presumably founded (at least in its European form) by Christian Rosenkreutz who lived around 1400 A. D. -- at the same time that Tzong-Kha-Pa was regenerating Buddhism in Tibet, and a mystic renas-

cence was about to be initiated in India by men like Raman-
anda, Kabir, Nanak and Krishna Chaitanya under the Sufi influence. The transition from the "ninth House" to the "tenth
House" phase of this movement can be seen in the spiritual
relationship between men like the great Benedictine abbot of
Wurtzburg, John Trithemius, 1450-1518 (who is associated
with the story of Faust), Cornelius Agrippa (1486-1503) and,
greatest of all, Paracelsus (1493-1541).

A few decades later, in England, this first phase of the
"tenth House period" has its striking manifestation in the
Elizabethean Age (1558-1603) and its great men who, at the
same time, accept a great deal of the spiritual-alchemical
thought of the Rosicrucians and initiate the new spirit of scientific experimentalism (Francis Bacon's and his Novu m
Organum) and of individualistic modern psychology (Shakespeare's Hamlet, etc.) --while in Italy, men like Bruno and
Galileo uphold the new vision of the world of which Copernicus has been the prophet.

With the second phase of the period -- 1613 to 1703 --
we witness the crystallization of the new spirit in the late
Renaissance and the Classical Era. And the most characteristic social phenomenon is the development under Riche-
lieu of the French authoritarian State symbolized by Louis
XIVth (le Roi Soleil) and the Court of Versailles with
its formalistic culture. French rationalism is characterized
by the philosophy of Descartes and by such literary figures
as Corneille, Racine, Moliere, La Bruyere, etc.

The triumph of French culture is established partly upon
the foundation of Germany's defeat and near-annihilation in
the Thirty Year War. The Peace of Westphalia (October 24,
1648) retards the development of Germany as a nation, and
thus can be said to be the foundation of the struggle between
France and Germany which will lead to the recent World
Wars. England, in the mean time, having enriched herself
by pirating the gold which Spain has been extracting from
America and the tortured Indians, is slowly building her

Empire. Spain is degenerating and Italy remains divided, Sweden rises to a momentary state of political hegemony; and the giant Russia, having repulsed the Mogols, awakens to Western civilization under the Romanovs (Peter, the Great; 1689-1725).

XI. 1702 to 1882 A. D.

This "eleventh House" period is fittingly an age of radical political, then social revolution and transformation. It can also be divided into two 90-year phases. From 1703 to 1793, we witness the political revolutions in America and in France, with their background of intellectual struggle against the authority of King and Church. From 1792 to 1882 the Western world experiences the momentous industrial and social-spiritual revolution which poses all the problems which confront our tragic twentieth century. The "political revolution" phase represents the involutionary descent of the new spirit; the "industrial revolution", the evolutionary ascent of new levels of humanity and of mental thought in answer to the challenges of this new spirit. Uranus (discovered in 1781) symbolizes the first phase; Neptune (discovered in 1846), the second.

The abstract (then emotional) idealism of these eighteen decades, the fervor and hopes and wishful dreams of the great Romanticists -- from J. J. Rousseau to Victor Hugo, from Thomas Paine to Fourier or Karl Marx, from the English Locke to the American Lincoln and the Russian Kropotkin -- the collective yearning to build a new world, and the seership of Prophets who envision new patterns of society; all these things (and their dark shadows: national imperialism, bourgeois greed and Victorian hypocrisy) are typical expressions of the eleventh House in astrological symbolism. To understand these historical phenomena as "eleventh House" characteristics gives to the astrologically minded historian a new insight in this crucial sequence of events and cultural developments. It adds a "new dimension of understanding", a cyclic dimension. And, using it, new and most significant historical correlations can be made.

For instance, we can compare the sudden spread of Islam during the fifth House period of the Piscean Age to the colonial imperialism of Europe during the eleventh House period, its astrological polarity. Dark Ages there were on the European continent, as the Roman Empire became completely liquidated and Asiatic peoples crashed the gates of Europe. A whole half-cycle later, it is Europe's turn to invade Asia and Africa; and the era of conflicting nationalisms and scientific materialism can also be considered a "dark" period from the point of view of the universalistic character of spirit. The great Catholic (i.e. universal) Order of the seventh, eighth and ninth Houses period (983-1523) thus is shown also to correspond to the Roman Empire of the cyclically opposite first, second and third Houses period of the Piscean Age (99 B.C. to 443 A.D.).

These and similar correspondences or polar relationships are not only significant in terms of a more coherent and vital understanding of the past, they enable us to orient ourselves toward the future, now in the making during the last of the twelve House-subdivisions of the Piscean Age, in which we are still living.

XII. 1882 to 2162 A.D.

During such a twelfth House period a double process operates more or less inevitably. On the one hand, the "karma" of the failures of the past (the sins of omission as well as of commission) is being precipitated along the lines long set by the momentum of ancient deeds and perversions; while on the other hand, this is the "seed period" during which the patterns of thought, feeling and behavior which will structure the coming Aquarian Age are being formed, focused within and released through the minds of a number of "seed men" in all fields of human activity.

As we are living now during this period and therefore we are most concerned with its meaning, an entire chapter will be devoted to it. Actually these 180 years constitute only the larger part of the period of transition between the Piscean and the Aquarian Ages; for, according to the ancient theory of cycles, such a transition should be said to last the final tenth part of the whole cycle. In this case, this means a 216 year period. If the Piscean Age ends around 2062, this transition period began in or around 1846. We could make it start in 1844, the time of the beginning of what is now known as the Baha'i Faith, the first world-religion actually to promote in a most definite and concrete manner a World-Order embracing the whole of humanity without any distinction of color, class, caste, religion, culture, or even sex. But we should not forget that the Communist Manifesto appeared in 1848 at the time of a revolutionary upsurge in Europe; and I shall tentatively show how it is possible to consider the Baha'i World-Order and World-Communism as the twofold polarization -- spiritual and materialistic -- of the inevitable planet-wide trend toward a global society; the first polarity being founded on universal Love, all-inclusive harmony and revealed "Truth"; the second, on violence, and the use of deceit and hatred as instruments of policy. Thus the year 1846, mid-way between 1844 and 1848 could be very significant.

It is certainly most significant to the astrologer, for Neptune was discovered on September 23, 1846 by Galle in Berlin. And Neptune is now believed to "rule" the zodiacal sign, Pisces. Thus the discovery of Neptune coincided with the beginning of the "seed period" concluding the Piscean Age, bringing, as it were, to the collective consciousness of mankind the announcement of the "c o n s u m m a t u m E st" -- the last words of Jesus on the Cross.

VII. AT THE GATES OF THE NEW AGE

In the first chapter of this book I showed how the discovery of Uranus, Neptune and Pluto in the eighteenth, nineteenth and twentieth centuries coincides with a threefold crisis of world-transformation. Many years ago in 1921, before I became seriously interested in astrology and before the discovery of Pluto, I wrote a book, never published, called THE AVATARIC CYCLE. In it I stated that these three centuries should be seen as a great drama in three acts, a drama whose theme was the coming of a new Avatar. Now I am inclined to think that the eighteenth century (called by some "the century of the lights") should be considered rather as a Prologue, and that the three Acts encompass the nineteenth, twentieth and twenty-first centuries.

What I wanted to show, nearly fifty years ago, was that we should not consider the coming of a great Avatar as a single event, but as a relatively lengthy process beginning with a revolutionary challenge to the old and obsolescent Order, and becoming a positive manifestation of the New Order successively at several levels. What occurs is a gradual "descent" of a new cosmic vibration, or rhythm and quality of being, affecting the whole of humanity, and indeed the entire planet, Earth.

At first this descent operates as a mental impact stirring the minds of individuals especially ready to act as critics of the past, but at the same time able to resonate to the archetypal patterns of a yet distant future. The seed-pattern (or archetype) of this future is then being sown in the

minds of a few thinkers under a guiding pressure from far
above their normal consciousness; and it is in the name of
this intuitional "sensing" of an as yet unclear ideal that these
individuals, and others aroused to action by them, begin to
act as catabolic agents, as destroyers of what the masses of
the people are still then taking for granted.

This first period should therefore be considered a Prologue rather than a First Act. It corresponds in our present historical period to the eighteenth century, especially
since the establishment of the first Masonic Lodge in London
in 1717. If one wanted to use the traditional Hindu symbolism of the Trimurti (or divine Trinity) we might call it
the Shiva Period, for Shiva is God in His aspect as destroyer
and purifier. Within or rather through the Shiva-fire --
which corresponds astrologically to Uranus, the iconoclast
and revolutionist -- one can already see the outline of the
fire; but this light will shine forth far more brilliantly during
the real First Act of the great planetary ritual-drama which
is the coming of the Avatar in whom the spirit of the "New
Age" is impersonated as a Prototype.

There must be an "impersonation" within (and especially
through) a human being because man can only become what
he is able to consciously imagine, and most men
must have some sort of model as a basis for their visioning.
There is always a Prototype in whom the Archetype in-car-
nates. Through him the creative Power, or Logos, which
makes possible the new cycle is released. He is both Exemplar (Form-aspect) and Source (Energy-aspect) -- and
this first manifestation of what is yet to come is followed by
a new release of Consciousness, perhaps a complex and multi-faceted release which nevertheless can also be related to
a central person or group of persons. After Shiva, we see
appearing the Brahma and the Vishnu aspects of the divine
creative Power.

The nineteenth century saw the revelation of the Brahma

power; which in Christian esotericism would be called the Father-aspect. Ancient occultism speaks always of the Hidden Father. But this hidden or occult character may be only relative. I spoke in the preceding chapter of the possibility that the Essene "Teacher of Righteousness" did represent the Father-aspect of the creative release which was at the source of the Piscean Age. If so, this personage was relatively hidden within a special group of devotees. This Father-aspect (or its "veiling" under a human Neptunian Form) could well have been in our present transition (or seed) period which will lead to the actual and concrete establishment of the Aquarian Age, the great Persian prophet, Baha'u'llah. He was seen and described in his full, majestic stature only by one Western traveler, Professor Edward G. Browne of the University of Cambridge. Professor Browne was able to have audience with Baha'u'llah at Bahji (near Haifa) in 1890, two years before the Prophet's death, and he recorded his impressions as follows:

"My conductor paused for a moment while I removed my shoes. Then, with a quick movement of the hand he withdrew, and, as I passed, replaced the curtain; and I found myself in a large apartment, along the upper end of which ran a low divan, while on the side opposite to the door were placed two or three chairs. Though I dimly suspected whither I was going, and whom I was to behold (for no distinct intimation had been given to me), a second or two elapsed ere, with a throb of wonder and awe, I became definitely conscious that the room was not untenanted. In the corner where the divan met the wall sat a wondrous and venerable figure, crowned with a felt head-dress of the kind called taj by dervishes (but of unusual height and make), round the base of which was wound a small white turban. The face of him on whom I gazed I can never forget, though I cannot describe it. Those piercing eyes seemed to read one's very soul; power and authority sat on that ample brow; while the deep lines on the forehead and face implied an age which the jet-black hair and beard flowing down in indistinguishable luxuriance almost to the waist seemed to belie. No need to ask in whose presence I stood, as I bowed myself before One who is the object of a devotion and love which kings might envy and emperors sigh for in vain!" (cf. BAHA'U'LLAH AND THE NEW ERA, p. 49, by J. R. Esslemont).

The twentieth century should now witness the manifestation during this transition period of the Son-aspect of the divine creative Power, the Vishnu aspect. This aspect refers to Consciousness -- that is, to the awareness (becoming increasingly spread out among men) of what is at stake, what is being built in the concrete minds of especially open and responsive individuals, here and there, everywhere. Our century is the century of "seed men". The Son is the central Seed-Image. It is the Christos, the God-Seed, p o t e n t i a l in every man, actually germinating and growing into plant and flowers in but a relatively few individuals. At the atomic and biological level it is the nucleus. At the psychological level it is the integral person, as an organized "field" through which divine power can become focused and is able to concretely act, or p e r-f o r m.

Why then do we see astrologically this twentieth century of ours symbolized by the awesome countenance of Pluto, ruler of the depths of existence? Because the unconscious depths of human existence must be aroused and purged, the ghosts of the past must be faced and dissolved by the "sword of severance" (which Jesus brought to collective mankind) b e f o r e the new seeds can begin to germinate -- perhaps under the symbolism of a trans-Plutonian planet which I long ago named Proserpine.

The zodiacal sign Pisces has a passive, receptive, "psychic" aspect; but it is also the sign in which the sword of severance can be handled to cut through the phantasms of accumulated and festering subconscious and karmic memories (or "engrams"). In the sign Pisces, many generals and admirals have been born, including Washington. As the last sign of the zodiac, it represents b o t h the karmic pressure of the past, and the great effort of repudiation and purgation needed to overcome this past. It is the symbol of collective crises, of group-catharsis. And when Pluto focuses its ruthless energy upon such crises, these indeed become awesome in their relentless and total character.

The conjunction of Neptune and Pluto in 1891-92 initiated the process which we see operating during this twentieth century. It began the new Electronic Revolution, with the discoveries of X-rays and radium, with the Quantum Theory -- and also with Freudian psycho-analysis which led to the proliferation of psychological systems and of techniques of psychotherapy. The release of atomic energy which began when Neptune entered Libra (first atomic pile reaction in Chicago December 1942) and the atomic explosions of 1945 were further manifestations of the capacity inherent in a consciousness attuned to the rhythm of cosmic energy to per-form in the creative-destructive mode of the Divine. God is focused in the infinitesimally small as well as in the immensely vast universal Whole. The release of God-power in perfect and total performances is the meaning of "divine Sonship".

This is why our century is one dynamized by "activism". It is a century of c o n s c i o u s n e s s b e c o m e a c t. But all releases of power are bi-polar. Every intense light casts an equally intense shadow. To a Sri Aurobindo and Gandhi answer a Hitler and Stalin. Likewise to the Bahai Faith envisioning a World-Order based on Love answered last century the World-Communism of Karl Marx fostering the war of classes and the ruthless "dictatorship of the proletariat". The two polarities of power and of consciousness are necessary within the ever-dynamic Harmony of the universal Whole.

The Forties of last century constituted undoubtedly a turning point. It focused the final aspect of the Industrial Revolution through the spread of railroads and the first telegraphic communication. It was the beginning of the Human-

itarian Movement which took various forms, whether in the
field of religious socialism (mainly through French leaders
like St. Simon, Lamennais, Fourier) or in that of medicine
and of spiritual healing (through disciples of Mesmer). It
saw the extraordinary spread of Spiritualism throughout the
U.S. and later in Europe. And it witnessed in May 1844 the
Declaration of the Bab in Persia, announcing the end of an
Age and the impending appearance of a great "Divine Manifestation" which would sound forth the creative Tone of a new
era of human evolution.

The story of the young, beautiful and fascinating Persian
youth Mirza Ali Muhammad, who took the name of the "Bab"
(meaning, the Gate) is an extraordinary one. It is detailed
in a remarkable book, THE DAWN-BREAKERS (Bahai Pub-
lishing Committee, New York). Thousands of his followers
were tortured and killed. He himself was put to death by the
fanatic Mohammedan clergy. One of these followers, Mirza
Husayn Ali (born in Teheran, November 12, 1817 exactly at
sunrise, and the son of a minister of the Persian Shah) was
thrown into a pestilential airless dungeon, chained with crim-
inals. There this man became aware of his status and he
was finally released thanks to the entreaties of the Russian
ambassador (an interesting connection!), and exiled with his
family and a few friends to Bagdad where he proclaimed his
status as a "divine Manifestation". Baha'u'llah was sent later to Haifa where he passed away. The tombs of the Bab
and Baha'u'llah are now located on the famous Mount Carmel
near the headquarters of the Bahai Movement.

This Movement spread to the Western world under the
leadership of Baha'u'llah's son, Abdul Baha, until after World
War I, then of a relative of both the Bab and Baha'u'llah,
Shoghi Effendi. After the latter's death a few years ago, the
movement is now directed by a group named "the Hands of
God", and it has centers in nearly every country of the world.
In Winnetka, near Chicago, a Bahai temple of remarkable
architecture is an extraordinary monument to the vitality of

this faith. The main emphasis in the Bahai writings is on basic principles of world-organization and interpersonal, communal, everyday relationships. The fundamental twelve principles of the New Order proclaimed by Baha'u'llah are (1) the oneness of mankind; (2) independent investigation of truth; (3) the foundation of all religions is one; (4) religion must be the cause of unity; (5) religion must be in accord with science and reason; (6) equality between men and women; (7) prejudice of all kinds must be forgotten; (8) universal peace; (9) universal education; (10) spiritual solution of the economic problem; (11) a universal language; (12) an international tribunal.

In contrast to the Bahai Image which radiates organizing power substantiated in love and peace, the Communist Image projected by Marx, and made triumphant some seventy-two years later by Lenin, has featured violence, deceit, and power without love -- sheer and naked power.

Power alone is not sufficient to produce a new world and a new society. What is inherent, but only potential, in the rhythm of power must be "per-formed"; i.e. it must operate through a steady and adequate form. Such a form is implied in the original release of creative power, but it has to be made explicit by a focused and structured human consciousness of a builder's mind. And this is where the Vishnu or Son aspect of the creative and transforming process comes in. I repeat that the great symbol of the beginning of this Second Act of the Avataric ritual-drama is the conjunction of Pluto and Neptune in 1891-92. These two years were those of the passing of H. P. Blavatsky and Baha'u'llah.

H. P. Blavatsky has been villified, and the Theosophical Movement of which she was the Source (a source, being a place through which water flows for external use by living entities) has had a very confused, twisted and often perverted career. Yet the effect of this Theosophical Movement, in all its forms, has had a tremendous, and often very little recognized influence upon the minds of fairly large groups of persons all over the world. Its basic implications -- the existence of super-human beings who guide the evolution of the planet and of mankind, and who can and do establish contacts with truly individualized, steady and open individual human beings -- runs counter to the exaggerated egocentric individualism of our times, as well as to the dogmatic beliefs and premises which limit the fields of modern scientific enquiry. Nevertheless, in one form or another, a truly sound, open, yet sharply discriminating and objective "theosophical" approach should be invaluable in solving those twentieth century problems which refer to the development of basic "seed-ideas". Such seed-ideas are necessary to serve as a solid, steadying and "cosmic" background for the performance of men who will act as builders of the new society.

When the Bahai writers speak of the building of a Bahai World-Order encompassing the whole of humanity and integrating science, religion, morality in a body of divinely revealed Laws and Precepts, they usually do not stop to realize that, unless our present society all over the globe collapses during some natural or man-made series of catastrophies, an immense number of exceedingly well-trained and spiritually lucid and courageous "builders" will be required to handle the controls of a highly technologized society. Such men could well be a special breed of ultra-modern technocrats which would rule over a global society under an expanded quasi-Fascistic regime. But they may also be spiritually conscious, dedicated and compassionate "Servants of humanity". How to produce such a vast "elite" of Servants of humanity is certainly the great problem of the present day and of many tomorrows. Such movements as the one initiated in Pondicherry, India, by the great philosopher-seer-yogi-poet, Sri Aurobindo, who at first fought for the liberation of India before Gandhi began his work, may show a way toward the formation of the required type of spiritually ded-

icated persons -- and the city of Auroville now being con-
structed as a "seed pattern" for many such future communities may well provide a remarkable example for the coming
generations. Various attempts by groups of young people
emerging from the "hippy" type of protest against our technocratized culture, and seeking to establish communities in
the Mountain States of the U. S. and in Canada, may be also
heralds of things to come.

All these quite recent efforts, following the conclusion of
World War II and the explosive release of nuclear energy,
are characteristic of the possibilities which should become
actual and steady facts during this last part of the twentieth
century; indeed before Pluto enters Scorpio and Neptune and
Jupiter enter Capricorn -- a very short time indeed! Yet
during these 15 years ahead of us, the young men and women
now in their early twenties and late teens will be reaching
their mid-thirties, a time for dedicated yet mature action.
Within the ten years that will follow (1984 to 1995) the fate of
humanity may well be decided -- or at least the manner in
which the new Aquarian Age will begin some 72 years later.

THE THREE 72-YEAR PERIODS: 1846 to 2062

In order to analyze more closely the character of historical events during the "seed period" of the Piscean Age we
can divide it into three sub-periods of 72 years duration. In
72 years (approximately) the equinoxes move back one degree of longitude in relation to the "fixed stars" and their
mythical constellations. As the constellation, Pisces, is
supposed to extend along 30 degrees of the s i d e r e a l zodiac, this means that in 1846 the vernal equinox was at the
third degree of the constellation Pisces. The equinox reached the second degree 72 years later in 1918, and it will reach
the first degree in 1990. These dates are obviously significant, for 1918 was the year World War I ended, one year
after the Bolshevik Revolution in Russia, led by Lenin; and
in 1990 there will be a gathering of many planets in the sign

Capricorn. On February 19, 1990, the Moon, Venus, Mars, Saturn, Uranus and Neptune will be in Capricorn, with Mercury just out of the sign. Jupiter will be moving through Cancer and Pluto through Scorpio. Six planets will indeed be found in Capricorn at various times during 1989 and 1990, and there will be a solar eclipse at Capricorn 25° in mid-January, 1991 close to Saturn.

1846 to 1918:

This is the age of nationalism, of industry, of colonialisation and of scientific materialism, the Victorian Age and its prolongation -- ending in the great catastrophy of World War I, which proved that the fears engendered in the minds of far-seeing men witnessing the first results of the Industrial Revolution in the Forties were indeed legitimate. But polar to this general trend we witness also the development of new religious, occult and humanitarian movements.

1918 to 1990:

The "war to end all wars", the "crusade for democracy" against German militarism turned out to be a futile tragedy, killing directly and indirectly many millions of young men. The Peace of Versailles and the repudiation by a handful of American Senators of the Wilsonian dream, the League of Nations, led directly to the rise of Nazism and Fascism -- and the senseless adoption of Prohibition produced in America both a nearly universal disregard of legality, and the growth of organized crime syndicates of unprecedented power. Above all, this period in which we are living is characterized by what really should be understood as "the Civil War of Man" -- the religious war, cold or hot, between Communism and Capitalism. This is an all-pervasive civil war, which recently has become somewhat altered, taking several aspects, mainly the struggle between the under-developed countries (the "Third World") full of nearly starving people and the richer nations which include not only the United States

and Western Europe, but Russia and her more or less obed-
ient "satellites". The struggle between the new generations
and the Establishment, in practically all countries, reveals
another aspect of our present schizophrenic, dichotomized
mankind. This condition was symbolized accurately in the
chart of the twentieth century (for January 1, 1900 - when the
new vibration of 19 superseded that of 18) and in the chart of
the solar eclipse of December 2, 1899. This last New Moon
of the nineteenth century saw seven "planets" in Sagittarius
opposed to the still close conjunction of Neptune and Pluto in
Gemini. I discussed these charts many years ago in the magazine AMERICAN ASTROLOGY, and they have been remarkably accurate in pointing to the great crises mankind has experienced since 1900. The strenuous aspects of Uranus and
Pluto in Virgo opposing Saturn in Pisces (1965-1966) squared
the basic opposition of the 1900 chart between Gemini and
Sagittarius. And we have had Vietnam, the Kennedy assas-
inations, the rise of Black America, the revolt of the young,
the monetary world-crisis, etc.

All this is leading inescapably to the third sub-period of
this epoch of transition between the Piscean and the Aquarian Ages. The great question is: what is just ahead now, before 1990? Will the entrance of Pluto in Scorpio in 1983-84
strike the gong for a planet-wide catastrophy -- just as Pluto's entrance in Cancer indicated the start of World War I
(with its prelude, the Balkan wars), and its entrance in Leo
marked the beginning of Hitler's conquest? When Pluto entered Virgo in 1957 the Russian Sputnik began the race to outer space and the Moon. Did this herald an as yet unclear
series of future crises?

In 1971 Pluto will reach Libra in sextile to a conjunction
of Jupiter, Mars and Neptune in Sagittarius, and in trine to
Saturn in Gemini. Will this mean a deeper sense of coop-
eration -- of will the opposition of Jupiter and Neptune to
Saturn during the summer-fall 1971 mark another kind of
dichotomy, perhaps related to the Jupiter-Saturn conjunc-

tion of 1961 which stamped the Kennedy Administration with a potentiality for tragedy?

1990 to 2062:

In view of the crucial all-human choice implied in this last question mark, it would be futile to try to foresee what this last 72-year phase of the Piscean Age will witness on this earth. The possibility of important telluric changes, perhaps of a sudden alteration of the polar axis or of the rise of at least a portion of a new continent is certainly not to be dismissed too lightly -- nor the possibility of contact with the "humanity" of another planet or solar system, a contact which could give a tremendous shock to the collective mind of earthly mankind. Yet it seems to be in the nature of our human race to seek external solutions to its ever-recurring problems, or some external answer to its never-ending questions.

I do believe in the intervention of the Greater Whole at crucial periods in the life-span of the smaller wholes which participate in Its vaster being -- and this possibility of intervention is no more startling than the immediate rushing of antibodies and white blood cells to any injured part of a man's body. Without having to subscribe blindly to the transcendental belief in a "Mystical Body of Christ" in which we live, move and have our being as individual human organisms, I see no reason to doubt the fact that the earth is a thoroughly "organized system of activities"-- even if we refuse to call it a "living organism" -- and that this planetary system (and the still vaster solar system of which it is but a part) has the power to readjust fundamental states of disequilibrium and perverted activities which endanger the dynamic balance of the whole system. We can speak of a t r a n s c e n d e n t God, but we probably do not need to speculate that far, for the c o s m i c reality of an organized solar system (or even of a planet) provides us with at least most of the answers we need to account for e x t r a - o r d i nary "interventions" in the affairs of mankind.

The only thing which makes such a type of thought unpalatable to our modern "scientific" mentality is its blind faith in so-called natural laws which represent at best but a narrow view of the ordinary behavior of the powers operating in the solar system and the cosmos. A reaction of the planet as a whole to the explosion of hydrogen bombs is, in principle, as explainable as the reaction of the stock market in New York to the start or the end of a war in Asia. Life can protect itself, and I have already shown (in the Prologue) how, with our narrow historical perspective and our very vague and sketchy geological understanding of the past of our globe (not to mention our totally speculative grasp of how the solar system was formed), we have absolutely no way of really knowing whether or not planets and solar systems are manifestations of a cosmic form of "life". There is really no more dogmatic statement than the assertion that our so-called "laws of nature" operate always and in any section of space as we think they do according to our earth-conditioned knowledge, limited as the latter is to an infinitesimally small moment of the existence of the cosmos.

This modern dogmatism becomes even more unjustifiable since we have built computers that "think" -- or at least that can react to abnormal situations and thereby preserve their integrity. At least we could think of the solar system as a gigantic computer able to re-adjust its basic harmonic patterns of existence when menaced by some destructive, centrifugal (and we might say "cancerous") development on the life-processes of one of its planets! By saying this, I do not belittle the validity of a belief in God or in god-like Agencies and superhuman Minds constituting the structuring and guiding aspect of planetary, or cosmic Wholes. A "cold" cosmic Power of Harmony able to readjust everywhere self-defeating states of acute disequilibrium may not be satisfying to the human mind which needs to feel "warmed" by emotions of love; but at least such a cold Power is thinkable and indeed should seem to any broad and non-dogmatic human intelligence perfectly understandable and "logical". Again, I repeat, Life everywhere is able to protect itself in one way or another. Why should it not do so at the planetary or cosmic level? Because we do not know exactly h o w it could do it at such levels certainly should not stop us from accepting the extreme probability of such a hypothesis.

HISTORICAL PARALLELISMS

Arnold Toynbee in his STUDY OF HISTORY draws at length structural parallels between the development of what he calls civilizations or Societies. Each of these is shown to pass through a series of recognizable and most characteristic phases of growth, maturation and disintegration. If he had been able or willing to combine the astrological with the historical-structural method he might have pin-pointed even more definitely the timing of the whole process of growth and decay of our civilization. It may be dangerous -- and, from the point of view of most of our contemporary historians trained in American universities, quite objectionable -- to think in terms of historical analogies between events occurring at the interval of over two millennia; yet this can be very suggestive, provided one does not try to take a narrow, literal approach which considers concrete events rather than s i g n i f i c a n t s t r u c t u r a l p h a s e s of the historical process.

In some instances the analogies are rather startling, even in terms of the appearances of great personages who have focused and embodied structurally inevitable trends of collective, cultural development. One of these analogies is the one paralleling the careers of Alexander the Great (356-323 B.C.) and Napoleon (1769-1821 A.D.) The city of Alexandria was founded in 332 B.C. and it became the great center of the Hellenistic culture, rivalling with Rome -- even after the battle of Actium (31 B.C.) which achieved the political control of Rome over the whole Mediterranean world.

Of course Alexander and Napoleon were entirely different individuals, and the concrete, factual events of their respective periods were totally unlike; but I am not thinking here, I repeat, of concrete events but only of phases of a structural process. Besides, the dramatic Play of the transition between the Piscean and Aquarian Ages is performed on a much larger stage than that existing 2160 years before. Also, as the last Act of the drama is not yet revealed, one cannot help being rather unsure of what is exactly happening today if this Piscean Age is, as I stated, Phase One of the great 25,868-year cycle. What occurred during its twenty-one centuries cannot correspond exactly -- even in terms of the over-all structural pattern of unfoldment -- to what happened during the Phase Twelve (so-called "Arian Age") of the preceding Great Sidereal Year.

For instance, the appearance of Jesus as the Christ probably a century after the start of the new Great Year refers, I believe, to this greater cycle as a whole more than to only its Phase One. The same is no doubt true of the appearance of Gautama the Buddha (and other great Teachers) in the sixth century B.C. These two great Personages, Gautama and Jesus, when considered as impersonations or concretizations of the cosmic Images of Christ and Buddha, belong respectively to the seed-ending and the germinal-beginning of two Great Sidereal Years. Their significance transcends the narrower scope of the twelve precessional Ages. The same might be true of Baha'-u'llah, though we may not have as yet a sufficient perspective on what he embodied in the evolution of mankind.

If we keep all this in mind, we can proceed with some degree of assurance in pointing out historical parallels which should help us to get a significant, even if largely tentative, picture of the meaning of our present historical moment. The parallelism, or the structural correspondences, refer to historical developments having occurred at an interval of about 2160 years. Thus the beginning of the transition be-

tween the Piscean and Aquarian Ages which occurred, as I
stated, in and around 1846 A.D. parallels the beginning of
the transition between the Arian and the Piscean Ages in and
around 315 B.C.

Both Alexander and Napoleon died only a few years before
the beginning of this transition (or "seed") period. They
cleared up the ground for the new process, by radiating southward and eastward some of the basic achievements of, respectively, the Hellenistic culture (Alexander in India) and the
French cultures (Napoleon in Egypt). Napoleon did not conquer the Anglo-Saxon world -- and therefore this world (especially England) is still unfortunately saddled with obsolete
types of measurements. Alexander did not conquer either
Rome and her Italian realm; but it was Rome which soon after conquered Greece and lastly Alexandria; and today we
see the United States, heir to the English tradition and basic
characteristics, slowly extending its grip over Western Europe, in a perhaps unstoppable process in spite of de Gaulle's
attempts or of efforts to consolidate Western Europe -- efforts paralleling after the death of Alexander the unsuccessful AEolian and Achaean Leagues; the old antagonism between
Athens and Sparta being at least partly responsible for this
failure. (Compare with conflict between France and Germany, or in another sense, France and England).

I have divided the transition period, 1846 to 2062, into
three 72-year sub-periods (representing one degree of precession of the equinoxes). The period 315 to 100 B.C. can
be similarly divided:

315 to 243 B.C. :
After Alexander's death in 323 his empire was divided
between his generals who fought against each other at least
until 277. This was followed in the Roman world by the first
of the three Punic Wars against Carthage, the first sea-pow-
er (264 to 24). 2160 years later sees the beginning of our
twentieth century. The Russo-Japanese War begins the cyc-

le of wars which are characterizing our centuries at the political-industrial level. The rise of Japan heralded the end
of the colonial system, and led to the rise of what now we
call the Third World. World War I began in 1914, or in fact
a few years before with the collapse of the Turkish Empire
and the Balkan Wars which followed.

243 to 171 B.C.

This period witnessed the Second Punic War in which
Hannibal's lightning moves and his elephants at first defeated
the Romans (compare with Hitler's blitzkrieg); but finally Rome won, and also defeated the Macedonians. This
72-year period sees the expansion of Rome from Spain to
Macedonia, Greece and Syria. It corresponds, I repeat, 2160
years later, to our present period, 1918 to 1990.

The great question mark of this present phase is raised
by the fact that two great "super-powers" have emerged,
U.S.A. and U.S.S.R. Obviously the world-stage has enormously increased, including now the entire earth; and the
production of atom bombs and of utterly devastating chemical
weapons has produced a situation totally unparalleled, or at
least seemingly so. It would be futile to expect future world-
events to correspond to what took place from 172 to 100 B.C.
and up to Caesar's death in 44 B.C.

The third 72-year sub-period of the present transition
between the Piscean and the Aquarian Ages begins, I repeat,
in 1990 as many planets are massed in the zodiacal sign,
Capricorn. It corresponds, 2160 years before, to 171 B.C.
The years following 171 B.C. see the last wars of Rome
against Macedonia and Carthage; then the beginning of a time
of civil wars in Rome between the have's and the have-not's
which ends only with Caesar and, after his death and the defeat of Cleopatra at Actium (31 B.C.), with the establishment
of the Roman Empire. The beginning of the Roman Empire
brings us, 2160 years later, to 2130 A.D.

Are we also "progressing" toward a now planet-wide and

equally ruthless Empire; and will it take that long to become established? No one can obviously answer such a question. One thing is certain: the tempo of history moves far more rapidly today than two thousand years ago, and armaments are far different from what they were. Yet, the very nature of these armaments might create a prolonged kind of equilibrium, and the Third World -- the new "Barbarians" within and without the dominant World-Power, or Powers -- may be contained for a long time.

On the other hand, the present world-policy of the U.S., under the very effective control of the "industrial-military complex" and with its "containment" principle, resembles very much that of the Roman Empire seeking also to contain the Germanic tribes along the boundaries of a (for the time) far-flung empire. But then we should remember that, at the end of a life-cycle, certain features which once prevailed at the beginning of that cycle tend to reappear. It has been remarked that the young Hippies of our day with their lovely, even if naive, stress on love and "flower power" resemble the early Christians in Rome. It may very well be therefore that the "Roman Empire" characteristics of the present-day United States -- and also in a more brutal way of the Russian Soviets -- are concluding imitations or repetitions of the imperial character of the Rome of the Caesars. So also was Mussolini's Italian Fascism a futile attempt to revive the Roman Empire on a limited scale; and Hitler's Nazi rule may remind us of Carthage and her worship of Moloch, the god appeased only by human sacrifices.

In other words, what may confront us today almost at the moment of the death of our Piscean Age is a resurgence of social-political-religious Images and collective behavior, which were developed during its infancy. These Images were actually the legacy of the great precessional cycle which ended around 100 B.C. -- i.e. the Images of the god-emperor inherited from Egypt and Persia, and the practice of enslaving or killing conquered people. These Images were brought to the Greco-Latin world in a new virulent form by Alexander when he tried to imitate the sumptuous Persian court, and by Caesar and his successors after conquering Cleopatra's Egypt.

Indeed a great law of retribution (karma) seems to be at work according to which the nation who conquers another by physical violence and wholesale death is in turn psychically conquered -- or at least deeply influenced -- by spiritual leaders of the conquered people. Just as the conquered Hebrews spread through Rome the Christian doctrine of Jesus and Paul, and defeated Rome psychically, so England conquered India, but the Anglo-Saxon world has become deeply influenced psychically by Hindu yogis and by Gandhi's movement of passive resistance. America defeated Japan, but Japanese architecture and the Zen doctrines are influencing today hundreds of thousands of Americans. While fighting the Barbarians, Rome opened herself to an inflow of Germanic mercenaries and to the new spirit of Nordic people; likewise, after having tried to contain Communism in Korea and Viet Nam, we already see a Korean "avatar" visiting us and perhaps establishing magnetic centers throughout the United States, and I foresee the probability of some Vietnamese movement spreading in the future to our land. An authoritarian Japanese movement, the Soka Gakkai, is already making many converts among Americans, and it is not impossible that this will be an important force to reckon with.

All this suggests that the present power of big business and militarism in the U. S. and in all the Western world, and also the Communist Party dictatorship (backed by the Army) are phenomena which represent the end of the Piscean Age. Whether they will be bequeathed to the new Aquarian Age next century remains to be seen. It need not be so; at least not in anything like their present form. It presumably will not be so if, as one may very well expect or envision, some radically transforming event occurs around 1990 on a planetary scale. A change in the earth's polar axis could even alter the length of the precessional cycle. A contact with super-intelligent beings from some other planet or solar system would also no doubt profoundly and radically affect man's mentality and presumably the entire pattern of human society -- which would then almost inevitably become integrated in opposition to, or in contrast to the newcomers from outer space. And, obviously, there could be a devastating nuclear World-War killing perhaps nearly half of mankind and making entire continents inhabitable for at least half a century -- perhaps until around 2062 A.D., the date I have given for the concrete, physical beginning of the Aquarian Age.

I certainly do not believe in the coming total destruction of the human race and the suppression of all possibilities of life within the earth's biosphere. I feel nevertheless that drastic developments are likely to occur around 1990 and after; and these might resemble, in a sense, the famed battle of Kurukshetra, which is described in the great Hindu epic, the MAHABHARATA. To this vast epic belongs the well-known Bhagavat Gita in which the incarnate Deity, Krishna, speaks to his disciple, Arjuna. In this battle of Kurukshetra which, tradition says, saw a confrontation between two equally matched armies, the rule of the Warrior Caste of ancient India was broken up. This opened the door to the domination of the Brahmin Caste and to the great Hindu "Age of Philosophy". It also marked the opening of the very vast cycle of Kali Yuga; and, as we already saw, it is said to have occurred in 3102 B.C. in the month of February. The Avatar, Krishna, was a great statesman, at least one aspect of whose work was the very destruction of the Warrior Caste.

For many years, I have felt that this was what was in store for mankind just now -- indeed since 1918. But of course we need not expect another Kurukshetra, or a Biblical Armageddon, or an apocalyptic and fiery Wagnerian consummation to our present Piscean Age. The fire may burn, but it also purifies. That the last 72-year sub-period from

1990 to 2062 will be a period of thorough and radical re-building seems a most likely possibility. Then the today so emotionally longed-for Aquarian Age should begin.

VIII. THE AQUARIUS-LEO AGE

At the beginning of Part Two I explained that the cycle of the precession of the equinoxes -- the Great Sidereal Year -- which lasts nearly 26,000 years and which we divide astrologically into twelve Ages is produced by the gradual retrograde displacement of the equinoctial axis, a displacement which becomes apparent when the position of the Sun at the time of the spring equinox is referred to some theoretically "fixed" star or group of zodiacal stars (i. e. constellations). The Sun does NOT enter the constellation Pisces or Aquarius in any particular century or year. It "enters" such a constellation every year; but it does so on a slowly but constantly changing day of the year. Each 72 years the Sun reaches the location in our sky of any particular prominent star near the ecliptic one day earlier -- which is another way of saying that the celestial longitude of that star increases by one degree every 72 years.

What "moves backward" with reference to the circle of our zodiacal constellations is the equinoctial axis. We must think of the two equinoxes as forming an axis, just as we must think of the Ascendant and Descendant of a birth-chart as the two ends (East and West) of the natal horizon. It is the equinoctial axis and not simply the vernal equinox which changes its position with reference to the stars. Thus, if one is to make any sense out of this motion, one must consider the displacement of two points, the spring and fall equinoxes, which are always in exact opposition. If the spring equinox is in Pisces, then the fall equinox must be in Virgo; and therefore to speak of the Piscean Age is to see only one side of the world-picture. We should always speak of the Pisces-Virgo Age. If I have not done so until now it is so as not to make the picture more complex. What is ahead of us this century is therefore not the Aquarian Age but the Aquarius-Leo Age.

In order to understand what this equinoctial dualism really means, let us consider afresh what the equinoctial axis represents. It is, as was stated on page 86 and 87, the line of intersection of two basic astronomical planes: the plane of the earth's equator and that of the ecliptic (i. e. the plane of our planet's orbit around the sun). These two planes form an angle of about $23°5'$. The plane of the equator refers essentially to the rotation of our globe around its axis; thus to the day-and-night cycle during which man experiences various levels of consciousness, from deep sleep to full waking consciousness. The ecliptic, on the other hand, refers to the year cycle, to the change of seasons. It deals with the constantly altered relationship between the earth's surface and the sun, source of the energies that operate within the biosphere and make life possible.

The day cycle sees an individual man's horizon being constantly altered. It symbolizes the many aspects of the consciousness and of the activity of a particular person; while the year cycle refers to seasonal changes which alter the rhythm of life itself all over the planet, and of course more specifically in regions not close to the equator. Thus one can consider the two equinoxes -- born of the relationship between the two planes and cycles -- as symbols of the way in which individual man is related to the rhythm of universal life which has its fountainhead in the sun; or the way in which the consciousness of man is related to the cyclically changing activities of life in a planetary sense.

This relationship of a particular type of man to the universal flow of life-energies on this earth is the root-factor in any culture or civilization. A culture refers to the response of a particular group of men (tribe, race, nation) to the basic conditions existing at any time and in any particular locality within the biosphere (i. e. on the earth-surface).

A "response" implies an activity to which one more or less consciously and deliberately reacts. One has to deal therefore with two factors, which can be symbolized as a "descent" of energy, and a responsive "ascent" of human consciousness and activity -- using of course the terms, descent and ascent in a symbolical sense. Thus, in astrology, the spring equinox refers to the descent of solar energy -- i. e. to the incorporation of creative, formative spirit -- while the fall equinox represents man's ascending toward an ever more effective and expanding consciousness of the meaning of universal life, according to the path traced, as it were, by the descent or incorporation of spirit (or logos).

The equinoxes may be considered as two "gates". At the vernal gate spirit enters into humanity and impregnates responsive human minds with great ideas, new rhythmic impulses, new "symbols of power". At the autumnal gate, individuals who have assimilated into their consciousness these creative gifts of the spirit and emerged from the womb of undifferentiated "human nature", rise, as individuals, to the divine Source and, in full consciousness, teach and embody into forms of understanding and of social relationship the Vision which "God" has bestowed upon them.

As I wrote many years ago, "the march of civilization is the march of earth-nature toward God -- through Man." But the positive factor in this onward march is the creative power of the spirit acting through ideas and impulses which thrill and fecundate humanity, causing great personages, who are mouthpieces of divinity and Fathers of civilization, to establish the foundations of new cultures in new or revitalized lands. Because this positive factor is represented by the vernal polarity of the equinoctial axis, it has been customary to speak, for instance, of the "Taurean" or "Piscean"

Ages. Yet, I repeat, such a practice is obviously inadequate; it restricts our understanding of what is really at stake, and particularly of the operation of cultural forces throughout a whole equinoctial Age. Indeed, by focusing the attention of the mind using the astrological tool of the equinoctial cycle upon the spiritually creative factor alone -- which is not productive of strictly speaking "cultural" manifestations -- a great deal of confusion has been caused as to what constitutes the "beginning" of an Age.

When the historial Oswald Spengler claimed that our Christian-European culture "began" around 900 A.D. with the spread of the Romanesque style and the birth of the great myths and legends which inspired poets and artists of subsequent centuries, he was right within the narrow limits of his understanding of the term "culture". Spengler, however, failed to grasp the meaning of the creative Impulse -- the "Christ Impulse" -- which is at the root of the Christian-European culture, because his absolute glorification of what he called "culture" made him blind to the positive meaning of "civilization". In its spiritual meaning, civilization refers to the universalistic creative Impulse of the spirit, and culture to the ascent of man (limited by particular earth-conditions) toward God.

THE PISCES-VIRGO AGE

If one considers what has been called the "Piscean" Age (which I have defined rather as Phase One of a complete cycle of precession) one should say that the Christ Impulse in it represents the Pisces factor or polarity, while the Romanesque-Gothic culture of the Middle Ages (from 900 A.D. onward) is to be linked to the Virgo pole. Indeed, we find the first centuries of this medieval period illumined by a worship of the Madonna, the Holy Virgin, and of all the Beautiful Ladies to whom Knights paid homage according to the spirit of Chivalry. The Christ spirit is that of the "fisher of men" out of the sea of the old equinoctial cycle -- Christ who stated that he brought to man the "sword" of severance from a concluded period of twenty-six millennia, rather than "peace". But the spirit of Chivalry and of the great cathedrals is to be seen as an expression of the Virgin's adolescent aspiration toward God, the Beloved -- a transcendent God not to be known concretely, a "dream lover" of the sky.

We cannot fully understand the Middle Ages in terms of Piscean symbolism, because during these centuries the dominant factor in Europe was not the "descent" of the creative Spirit, but instead the "ascent" of man. And this emphasis upon "ascent" has been retained by the men of the Renaissance and the builders of our classical science and philosophy, from Descartes to Darwin. Even today Western thought can hardly conceive evolution except as a straight line of ascent from barbarism to enlightenment, from amoeba to man. It stresses the evolution of earth-substance and physical organisms; and it ignores the "involution" of creative spirit through impulses and ideas which build civilization and all universalistic concepts or institutions.

In other words, at the beginning of an Age, the positive characteristics of this Age manifest in terms of the spring equinox polarity, while at and after the mid-point of the Age (about 900 A.D. in the "Piscean" Age) it is the fall equinox polarity which assumes the controlling role. Both are operative throughout the entire Age, it is true; yet during the first half of the Age the dominant historical fact is that universal spiritual values seek incorporation in the substance of the new humanity. By contrast during the second half the elite of this (then) spirit-impregnated humanity is striving to radiate outward and Godward through adequate cultural forms. These cultural forms are "man-made"; the revelations of the new spirit seeking to impress themselves upon the collective mind of the human races during the first half of an equinoctial Age are "God-inspired" -- whatever exact meaning we wish to give to the term, God.

The Gospels, we might say, were divinely inspired and

revealed through illumined personages. But the Catholic Church, as an institution which controlled the culture of Christian Europe, grew to its stature -- particularly thanks to the Popes Gregory I (600 A.D.) and Gregory VII (1075 A.D.) -- as an attempt by eminent individuals to build concrete social-religious structures that would powerfully show forth the glory of the divine Revelation. If early Christianity and the Roman Empire which built its power upon the mastery of the sea ("mare nostrum"), have a deep affinity with the symbolism of Pisces, the spirit of the Middle Ages and of typical European achievements by individuals is essentially of the nature of Virgo. Intellectual analysis, criticism and scholasticism (the foundations of European mentality) are all Virgo traits. Virgo emphasizes also the keynote of the European era, the factor of psychological crisis.

European man is characterized by Spengler as the "Faustian man" -- with reference to Faust, the restless seeker for truth, fulfillment and mastery, who made his famous pact with the Devil for the sake of regaining his youth. Faust, and also Hamlet, are men filled with a poignant sense of personal crisis. They are men either going somewhere at all cost, or unable to go anywhere because they cannot meet the cost of maturity and liberation from ghosts. European man has either sought the technique that would give him mastery even at the sacrifice of feelings and morality, or felt himself accursed by past failures he could not overcome. He has been essentially a technician or a sick man, and at heart a restless and forever dissatisfied individual, always ready to storm the gates of Heaven, or to rape ancient lands and peoples, or to collapse into a hopeless sense of sin and perdition; a man faced constantly by crises, which he solved Godward or hellward.

This psychological attitude was in no way that of the citizen of ancient Rome, or of the early Christian with his soul aflame with a strange glow of transcendent love, of destiny,

of newness of being. The Faustian-Hamlet type and the Ro-
man-Christian type are indeed as much polar opposites
as Virgo and Pisces are polar opposites. But in this case
Pisces comes first; it is the action to which Virgo is the reaction -- for we are dealing with a reverse or retrograde
zodiacal sequence. Moreover, if we want to grasp fully the
meaning of this action and this reaction we should remember
that both are expressions of Phase One of the 26,000 year
long precessional cycle.

It is because the Christian devotee of a transcendent yet
immanent God-Man and the Roman citizen of the first con-
sciously-built universalistic Empire were both pervaded with
the conviction that they participated in the establishment of
a truly new departure in human affairs, that their
distant European progeny (especially in Nordic lands) felt
burdened as individuals by a sense of personal crisis. The
men of the first centuries after Christ were participants in a
ritual of world-renewal of which Jesus-Christ was the Offic-
iant; but the men of the Middle Ages and the early Renaissance were individuals who had to take a tremendous step in
their personal lives -- now or never, at once, irrevocably.
If they were intensely Christian, they had to become saints
or be damned forever. If they were more intellectually and
individualistically oriented, they had to solve crucial psychological or scientific enigmas, or else become lost in insan-
ity or moral failure. In any case, they had to make an almost inhumanly critical choice, because they were to set the
pace for an entire world-cycle, or drop into the past as
failures.

Christ sounded a new keynote for humanity. It was so
new that the individuals who had to live by it were faced with
a truly tragic personal choice between tomorrow or yester-
day; and it is the essence of the Virgo phase of a cycle that
it revolves around the necessity for such a choice. Because
the Piscean Age is Phase One of the Great Sidereal Year, it
could be the beginning of the new evolutionary tide only in an

archetypal or transcendent sense, for in the first period of any spiritually considered cycle the weight of memories makes it difficult for the "new spirit" to be an actual power in concrete living. Generally speaking, Christianity has indeed presented the "way of Christ" only in an ideal and transcendent manner, as something to orient oneself toward, not actually to live by -- this, remarkable exceptions notwithstanding. Likewise the Roman Empire was a ruthless military autocracy far more than a truly universal organism in which all human beings could participate. It was based on Law, not on Harmony -- a fundamental difference of crucial importance at this time when, at the close of this Age, the same trends which gave to the Roman Empire its Fascistic character are at work, making an often tragic mockery of the spiritual Masonic ideal of democracy -- of "liberty, equality, fraternity".

As we now approach the Phase Two of the great cycle, the ideal should become reality, the transcendental divine must become incorporated into the planetary human; and the entire earth -- the one home of mankind -- is to demonstrate in actual reality the universal order of the sky. How can this be accomplished? By the release (or "downflow") of new spiritual-cosmic energies which, as they pervade and impregnate the earth's biosphere will trans-substantiate the materials of nature and of the human psyche, and as well precipitate as matter of a new type. If matter can be transformed by the Virgo-oriented minds of human scientists into tremendous releases of energy, so can new types of energy become apprehended as matter -- but not necessarily matter of a type which our present-day senses are able to perceive directly -- once this energy acquires a steady whirling rhythm.

In the astrological symbol of Aquarius, Man carries on his shoulders an urn from which "living waters" flow. These waters are contained within a formed structure, viz. an urn. What the modern seeker after mystical awareness often forgets is that power which is not contained within a form -- i. e. some kind of "engine" -- is ineffectual, and usually "wild" (i. e. untamed) in its explosiveness. This problem of "form" is indeed a dominant one today. A number of far-seeing scientist-philosophers realize this. The Gestalt School of philosophy approached the problem. Lancelot L. Whyte in his splendid book ACCENT ON FORM (1954) formulated it convincingly. I have tried for forty years to present it in terms of music and art, and later astrology -- for true astrology is the study of structures in time and space (i. e. of cycles and configurations).

The second phase in any kind of twelvefold zodiacal or House process has in astrology the character of being "fixed". There are three essential types of release of power: straightforward, circular (as in a whirlpool) and spirallic (a combination of the preceding two). These three types are given the names, respectively, of cardinal, fixed and mutable. In the "natural" seasonal zodiacal cycle, the first sign is Aries; it is cardinal, impulsive -- a release of germinal, originating power emerging with the compulsive drive associated with all evolutionary mutations, all "transpersonal" creative acts. But when we deal with the cycle of precession of the equinoxes, the process operates in an inverse direction, because the motion of the equinoctial axis is retrograde. Moreover, the frame of reference for the measurement of this equinoctial movement is constellations found along the ecliptic (i. e. the yearly path of the Sun in apparent motion in the sky), and not signs of the zodiac.

What I have been saying, I repeat, is that the retrograde motion of the vernal equinox through the constellation, Pisces, constitutes Phase One of the 26,000-year long precessional cycle. As the vernal equinox reaches the constellation Aquarius, Phase Two of the cycle begins -- the Aquarius-Leo Age. The type of energy-release during that Age is "fixed"; it forms vortices; and it is this type of energy which can in-substantiate itself as the primordial units of a new type of material existence. It may not be possible, however, for our senses as normally constituted today, to perceive this new type of matter; yet there are undoubtedly many people who at this time are born with super-normal powers of perception. We call them, rather indiscriminantly, clairvoyants -- indiscriminately, because what is widely known today as clairvoyance can mean a great many things, most of which do not refer to what I am discussing now, and because these "clairvoyants" are usually not reliable.

THE AQUARIAN FECUNDATION

The first thousand years of the New Age should constitute the predominantly Aquarius phase of that Age, while the second thousand-year period will be under the "influence" of Leo. This second period will be the r e s p o n s e of mankind to the descent of the Aquarius fecundation and revelation. The descent of new p o w e r will be "Aquarian", the consciousness and the future culture of mankind will have a Leo character.

This is very important because when we speak of the new Aquarian type of person, we are actually referring to human beings t h r o u g h w h o m will be released in some more or less focused and characteristic manner the energies, the faith, the downflowing enthusiasm and revelations of the new Age. These are dynamic features, and they refer to a large extent to unconscious or semi-conscious processes which occur t h r o u g h the individual persons rather than f r o m them. These true "Aquarians" can be placed in the category of "apostolic" men and women. They are mouthpieces for the new spirit, and many of them may almost be called born "mediums" for the release of that spirit at the beginning of the new cycle. In this they differ rather fundamentally from men who, as "seed men", constitute the harvest of the Piscean Age during the very last stages of that now ending cycle.

Apostolic men are animated basically by an intense fervor and act as power-stations or radiating centers -- and these were the characteristics of early Christians, and today already of most of the Bahais and of people "fascinated" by some new prenatally Aquarian movements. They constitute collectively the "germ" of the barely emerging plant -- some can be identified as parts of the symbolic rootlet that anchors the new emergence into the humus of the past. Their focus of expression is NOT the mind. They are indeed ruled by emotions of a certain type, and apostolic faith and self-consecration is of course an intense emotion, irrational or supra-rational in nature. They are people aglow with a radiation of "love -- often not intelligent and not controlled -- which can destroy as well as transfigure. They radiate a vision, a total conviction, a fire of the almost totally polarized psyche -- polarized by an irrevocable dedication which may lead to martyrdom. They are totally future-oriented.

On the other hand, seed-men are essentially synthesizing minds, but minds that are filled with the vital essence of a whole cycle, minds that operate in terms of what elsewhere I have called "eonic consciousness", that is, in terms of a consciousness that can survey a whole cycle of existence and human history, that is basically s t r u c t u r a l in its approach to life and all life-events, and in which the a l p h a joins the o m e g a in a process of creative synthesis. They too are future-oriented, but not in the same way as apostolic men. Their minds are filled with a vision, but if they are truly seed-men this vision does not express itself in outer action as much as in the formation of symbols -- and words, pictures, rituals, music are symbols. They deal only secondarily with personalities, for they are primarily intent upon a basic representation, reordering and transformation (metamorphosis) of the structures of consciousness. Apostolic men, coming after the New Age has begun (at least at a higher level of reality) disseminate the vision of the seed-men, or spread the creative words of the Avatar or Avatars.

Seed-men, whenever they appear today, constitute the ultimate expression of the Piscean Age, yet they hold within them collectively as a sacred essence the life-flame or the vibrant tone which, when released fully, will power the start of the Aquarian Age. They are not culture-oriented, and certainly not Establishment-respecting men. They herald the future culture; but only in so far as some of the basic structural and mental characteristics of this culture are concerned. It is in this sense that, for instance, Aristotle, Plato, and the Hebrew prophets can be considered quasi-"genetic" factors which operated as conditioning agencies in the building of the Christian-European mind.

We can have really no idea of what the predominantly Leo culture of a thousand years ahead of us will be. It will be determined by the manner in which mankind will respond, after next century, to the downpour of "Aquarian waters". As I already suggested, this response could operate in two very different ways according to whether our present technological society and its technocratic rulers (the real ones, not those pasted on the facades of our institutions) will collapse very soon under either internal and external pressures, man-made or telluric -- or else it will maintain itself for a relatively long time by the use of military and police power (served by physicists, chemists, biologists, psychologists, etc.) as the old Roman Empire did.

If the first alternative is at least basically correct, then a much less congested humanity having experienced a crucial catharsis on an earth-surface definitely altered, will have to recover from the "shock treatment" along various lines. A great world-religion will probably have emerged, having absorbed materials and ideas from old disciplines and ideologies. It would be attuned to the need of the masses. It would serve as the indispensable structuring and cementing force needed to gradually reorganize mankind-as-a-whole on a global scale. There would emerge also a number of "Gnostic" communities in many places which would be dedicated to the multi-faceted transformation of human beings, and which would radiate the higher expression of the Aquar-

ian spirit. It is among such communities that the genesis of
the future Leo type of individuals, and of the great myths and
culture of the Leo hemicycle of the New Age is most likely
to take place.

AN AGE OF MANAGEMENT OF POWER

It is fashionable today to think -- or rather to d r e a m!
-- of the Aquarian Age as an age of wonderful peace and spirituality, indeed as a utopian Millenium. If I am right in thinking of this coming Age as Phase Two of the Great Sidereal
Year, such a dream seems to be quite unrealistic and indeed
greatly misleading. The Phase Two of a cycle should witness, I repeat, the substantiation and concretization of the
ideals and the spiritual impulse which could manifest during
Phase One only in a transcendental manner. What I call
"the Christ Impulse" (cf. my book FIRE OUT OF THE STONE)
produced a relatively few great personages aflame with
"a g a p e-love" -- the most publicly known being probably
St. Francis. But this new Christ-power was not able to make
of Europe a Christically organized society; nor could the
wisdom and infinite compassion of the Buddha and of later
Boddhisattvas really transfigure the societies of India and
China. Jesus spoke essentially to individuals, and o n l y to
individuals. He was content to let Caesar take care of the
organization of the Mediterranean world, thus accepting im-
plicitly the dochotomizing of society into a sacred and a pro-
fane sphere, controlled respectively by Church and State.

This has some advantages, because by creating inevitable conflicts between the two spheres of power (for instance
Pope and Emperor during the Middle Ages) it gives more
chances for smaller groups and individuals to develop as
relatively free agents. We see the same process operating
today in relation to the "cold war" in which two national super-powers are stalemated, allowing for some freeplay among
smaller nations. If, however, this new Phase Two of the
great cycle having its spiritual source in the Christ-Impulse

of two thousand years ago, is to see the concrete actualization of what such an Impulse implies, a new situation will
have to develop. The key to such a situation may be found
in the often used motto "unity in diversity", which perhaps
would be more significantly phrased as: unity through diversity.

The point is that we are dealing here actually with two
factors: power and consciousness -- a dualism greatly stressed in the Tantric philosophy of India. "Power" in the coming Age refers to the Aquarius polarity (the vernal equinox);
"Consciousness" to the Leo polarity (the fall equinox). The
kind of power which will be consistently used during the coming Age may differ entirely from the type of energies which
we produce today by destroying a variety of materials (wood,
coal, oil, atoms), thus leaving inevitably a residuum of highly toxic waste-products poisoning slowly the whole biosphere. It may be power produced by tuning in, or resonat-
ing to a unitarian flow of cosmic energy pulsing rhythmically
through space -- power also related to what is the essential
or "divine" source of what we know at a lower level as "imagination" and "will" (in the old Hindu system, of kriyashak-
ti and Ichchashakti) -- power also related to "sound"
and its effect upon the formative agencies which structure
and control all existential concrete wholes.

Whatever is the source or nature of such powers, the essential point is that they have to be managed. And I believe that the problem of managing enormous powers potentially awesome in their effect will be the fundamental problem of the first half of the Aquarian Age. It is, of course,
already the fundamental problem of the coming decades of
this century. This problem -- as I pointed out in a book in-
adequately titled (by the publisher) as MODERN MAN'S CON-
FLICTS: The Creative Challenge of a Global Society (Philosophical Library, New York 1948) -- is twofold. "The demo-
cratic reliance upon the individual person must stay; but total productivity on a global scale must be established for all

men, and also in all men -- thus by all men. The values arising from the five-century old development of nations as cultural fields for the integration of diverse races, and superseding those of archaic societies based on the tribal ideal, must be retained in a form purified from political exclusivism and from the fallacy of the principle of absolute sovereignty; but atomic power must become the foundation of a global economy and an all-human world-society which will leave no one out and will discriminate against no race, no class, no group.

"These two pairs of apparent opposites can only be reconciled as the man of tomorrow harmonizes within himself the still more basic conflict between the ego, structuring his conscious life and his newly acquired sense of individual responsibility as a self, and those powers which, because they are rooted in the usually unconscious depths of man's common humanity, belong, not to the individual, but to Man as a whole." (Page 5).

The necessary requirement for the management of power which, by their nature and their potential for total destruction, can safely belong only to Man-as-a-whole is a highly centralized organization of controls, such as for instance we find in the nervous systems of a human being. As Oliver Reiser has repeatedly pointed out in his books dealing with the global organization of mankind (THE WORLD SENSORIUM, THE INTEGRATION OF KNOWLEDGE, COSMIC HUMANISM, etc.) -- and as Teilhard de Chardin suggested when speaking of the development of the noosphere of the earth -- mankind represents in a sense a planetary type of brain within which consciousness operates. As I have stated, it is Man's function within the earth-sphere to extract consciousness from all the activities being performed within the biosphere and above it. So far a divided mankind has been able to do this only partially through local and specialized, often sharply conflicting, societies and cultures. Now Man's performance is reaching the global stage. A global society must be organized structurally in such a way that production, distribution and consumption are harmoniously and almost automatically balanced and flow rhythmically through the entire earth-field. How can this be achieved? This is the great problem.

We can imagine conceptually a society in which this balancing and a complete adequacy of fulfillment to need has become an automatic operation -- one that is regulated as efficiently as autonomous functions and instinctive response to everyday challenges are effectively interrelated in a human organism. Various sections of our industrial output are already becoming organized at a national level in such a manner -- for instance, the release of electric power to meet a strongly varying demand for use according to the time of the day and of the year. But this type of organization still lacks a fool-proof stability and efficiency. Moreover it is at the mercy of conflicts between classes, ideological-political groups and nations -- conflicts which, in this sense at least, parallel neurotic psychosomatic symptoms or even psychosis in individual human beings.

To translate such already enormously complex systems of control, balance and feed-backs into a totally global system would assuredly require a most centralized type of authority and the absolute power to enforce its decisions. Could this operate while the inalienable freedom of the individual person and the diversity of racial, cultural, religious, political systems are considered to be absolute requirements? I personally cannot envision any way in which this could be achieved, UNLESS the concepts of individual freedom and cultural or group diversity are transferred from the realm of power (which really means, in the broadest sense, "politics") to that of consciousness. As long as the concept of politics remains a driving force among men, the only global society I can imagine is one based on some form of totalitarianism -- which means, as long as our present type of civilization exists, a technocratic type of control, i. e. the rule of managers and technicians operating through ever more complex types of machines and by means of psychological, biological and medical techniques.

Today the ordinary citizen is not normally concerned by the way an electric network of power-stations, or the international telephone or mail service, are run. It is conceivable that all social services, and perhaps even the production, distribution and consumption of food or other so-called "necessities", might eventually be run also in such a nearly automatic way -- i. e. without the intrusion of politics; which, in turn, means without the display in human beings of the will to power and of the craving for individualized profits that are measurable by wealth. It is conceivable; but is it likely to happen within the next two thousand years? When one looks at the mentality of the mass of human beings everywhere, one wonders.

What seems to me more likely is that the very basis of our science, our technology, our way of programming social existence will be altered. It may not be altered rapidly by man-made wars and revolution or by telluric upheavals. It may not be altered everywhere at the same time. There may be "germinal groups" co-existing with an increasingly deteriorating technocratic Establishment, whether at the global, or only at the national level. It is not even inconceivable that the parallel to a Roman Empire after the beginning of the Aquarian Age will be a network of deeply spiritually intent groups and communities whose members will not only intellectually, but occultly or "telepathically", realize their unity as components of the global organism of MAN -- while the "Barbarians" will be represented by the power-greedy politicians, the intellectuals, the worshippers of university-knowledge and of machine-technology. The roles may thus be reversed, but eventually the followers of the old order would become spiritually fecundated by those groups which they probably would have tried to destroy, as Germanic tribes became Christianized and transformed by the symbols, the language, the social concepts and to some extent the manners of those they conquered.

We can see such processes operating on a small scale even now. If mankind were to be shocked by some vast holocaust and continental upheavals, anything of course could happen; and it probably would not happen everywhere in the same way. But, whatever happens, the dream of an ideal, utterly spiritual and peaceful Aquarian Age seems to me an extreme illusion. A very gradual use of new powers by men whose consciousness will be deeply transformed by the very use of these powers seems inevitable. The great problem is likely to be the dissemination of these new powers through men whose consciousness and emotional drives would have to be so deeply re-oriented that the use of these powers by the average man and woman would be harmonious and constructive in terms of the unity of mankind.

Might not this take many centuries, perhaps millenia? It should be clear that any new technological advance which can be, and most inevitably would be used by the representatives of the old dying Order can only lead eventually to monstrous results. The Nazi system was (or should we not say "is"?) a reappearance of the old tribal Order based on the exclusivistic glorification of a particular race, land and folk-culture and religion. What this archaic philosophy of race and human evolution was able to do with an up-to-date technology is well-known. It is always the same when a primitive, animistic, frustrated and irrational mentality is given tools and powers produced by analytical and un-moral techniques based on a principle of destruction. The end-result is inevitably, sooner or later, self-destruction.

The new Age cannot begin until at least the most obvious and frightening aspects of our present-day technology -- in psychology as well as in physics, chemistry and biology -- are eradicated. Whether they can be eradicated by peaceful methods -- except here and there under special conditions --

is most doubtful. I firmly believe that it is to be hoped that the "eradication" will be done by agencies greater and more powerful than mankind -- and particularly by the earth itself whose energy-releases can far transcend our atom bombs. Telluric upheavals should certainly be much preferable to a world-wide nuclear holocaust. The re-orientation of our polar axis could indeed be a powerful means to bring about, at least indirectly, the re-orientation of Man's mind and consciousness -- and the resulting change in the concept of and the feelings related to social organization. But, of course, geographical and climactic changes would be only one aspect of the transformation. Man himself must accept and effectuate the transmutation of his mind and his vital-emotional energies. Our entire civilization and its institutions, our most basic attitudes to human relationship, our science and our education must be radically revaluated and oriented toward new goals. It must be transfigured by a "new" (as far as the average human being is concerned) realization of the place Man occupies in the universe and of Man's relationship to the creative force of this universe.

THE REORIENTATION OF CONSCIOUSNESS

Such a reorientation and repolarization of human consciousness evidently operates in various ways and under the pressure of different types of circumstances, personal or affecting at once large groups of people. There are today many groups in all countries who are striving more or less intelligently and wisely to effect such a transmutation -- perhaps the most notable one being the movement radiating from the Sri Aurobindo's ashram in Pondicherry, India under the leadership of the "Mother", a French woman of most unusual character. In many instances, however, such groups do not clearly understand the nature of some of the required first steps, because they operate much too much on a sentimental, over-idealistic and purely devotional basis; and some of them are unnecessarily dogmatic and depending on a quite blind belief in supernormal agencies for the transformation, whether these agencies are imagined to be super-human Adepts on this earth or "Space-people".

In such cases, a lack of historical perspective is usually evident, and also a true philosophical-cosmic foundation, which belief in supernatural "phenomena" can never replace, if really constructive results are to be expected. Before any constructive approach can be firmly developed, there must be a thorough and radical reorientation of the mind, and this means a critical evaluation of what today, in our Western society and over most of the globe, passes for "progress". This may well entail a nearly total repudiation of the so-called advantages and the comforts of modern suburban living; and some of the young men and women, more or less related to the "hippy" movement, are showing us the way -- especially those who are gathering in small communities in the Mountain states or elsewhere, living the hard existence of pioneers and attempting to develop a new spirit and new forms of interpersonal relationship.

It seems essential for all individuals who claim to strive after an "expansion" of consciousness to realize, and to totally accept the realization, that our science, our psychology, our traditional interpersonal behavior, and as a result our social, political and cultural way of doing things has developed in a "wrong" way. To understand why this way can only lead to destructive results in a more or less distant future -- perhaps a very near future -- requires a deep reorientation of consciousness as well as a transmutation of the basic energy-drive of the modern personality, dominated as it is by the ego and its wants, artificially stimulated by the dominant incentives and the competitive patterns of our society. Of course, for many centuries spiritual Teachers and mystics have urged men to overcome their instinctual appetites and emotional desires for ego-satisfaction; but now our whole society and our scientific-technological outlook in all fields of "research" are dominated by the wants of the

personal ego and the drives for ever more comfort and for
self-indulgence in every conceivable way. The real issue
therefore is more hidden, for external abundance can hide
far more effectively spiritual poverty or mental perversion
than scarcity and the concomittant effort necessary for wholesome survival.

This is not to say that such a development of the analytical intellect and the sharply individualized ego-consciousness
should never have taken place; indeed it was presumably necessary, because this is the way man has to learn, i. e. by
treading the path of self-destruction (the via negativa) --
up at least to a "critical state" beyond which there would be
no possibility of readjustment. But what is at stake now is
the realization that there is another way of releasing vast
amounts of energy for man's use -- a way which does not involve the destruction of matter, and thus the inevitable release into the biosphere of poisonous waste-products. It is
a "natural" way; but one which demands a radical revaluation of what man is as a total organism, and of his
relationship to the creative forces of the universe, i. e. to
spirit and to the Greater Whole within which we live, move
and have our essential being.

I repeat: the coming Aquarian first half of the coming
Aquarius-Leo Age will inevitably be an era consecrated to
the release and the control of "new" powers available to the
men and women who are ready to deal constructively with
them because they have radically re-oriented their minds and
transmuted their vital desires and their ego-polarized intellect -- who have gained a "new mind". This transformation
is not essentially unlike the metanoia preached by John
Baptist 2000 years ago; but it has now to operate within the
context of a far more complex and far more intellectual technological society. It requires therefore a new approach, perhaps greater courage and, above all, a greater lucidity and
objectivity of mind.

To the new man will be revealed new powers -- powers

that have always been there -- in his nature and in the earth's greater Nature. It will no doubt take centuries to learn to build a totally new culture on the basis of the use of such powers. I firmly believe that most of the efforts made by intellectuals and technicians to build up the new science of "prospective", and to extrapolate present trends into the future, are doomed to futility, at least as far as the next century and presumably the very last years of this century are concerned. The future presented to us by most writers of science-fiction is also a rather pathetic parody on what should develop during the coming thousand years. It reveals but too often -- exceptions notwithstanding -- a total lack of understanding of the possibility of transformation open to Man, which is caused by a rather blind dependence upon and the over-valuation of our modern scientific and technological mentality.

It is quite futile -- I repeat -- to try to guess at the manner in which the Aquarian descent of new powers will take place. As I already stated, I believe that great changes will begin to occur soon, and much may have happened by 1990 -- even if what is happening is not acknowledged and even less understood by the official mind and the Establishment; for, inspite of all the modern means of communication, much can indeed happen which remains unpublicized and, if known, is totally misinterpreted. The vast number of rumors and contradictory statements, of fairly incontrovertible observations and evident fallacies, of official denials from the government, and of mediumistic "communications"(supposedly emanating from Space-people) may be a good instance of the confusion prevailing during a period of transition during which an obsolescent social-political structure and the as yet inchoate upsurge (or downflow) of new types of power and consciousness interpenetrate at nearly all points.

It is, however, most important to realize, at this very moment of human history, that it is always BEFORE a new cycle opens that the "seed ideas" for the early development

of this cycle are released and sown into some at least relatively new -- or rather re-virgined -- soil. It is BE-
FORE the New Age opens that the new creative impulse, the
fecundating logos spermatikos, "descends" from the
divine realm into one man, and secondarily a group of men,
who incorporate it and make it manifest at least to a particularly open and responsive "creative minority".

However, the present widespread expectations for a new
Avatar may not correspond exactly to the actual historical
reality, for it seems very likely indeed that, as I already
stated, we are dealing now with a multi-levelled planetary
process extending over four centuries, and that there can be
"Avatars" at these several levels, -- possibly with reference to several cycles whose beginnings are nearly coincid-
ing. The Aquarius-Leo Age may not be the larger of such
cycles.

The future of Man indeed is wide open. It serves no very
valid purpose, I believe, to see this future through rosy glas-
ses compensating for inner fears and emotional insecurity.
The Aquarius-Leo Age will be an age of power and of totally
managed productivity at all levels. But it will no doubt be an
age in which the potential of spiritual and creative individuality hidden under the symbolism of Leo will, in due time
-- not at once -- blossom forth.

Humanity is unfolding its vast potentialities through a
Great Sidereal Year whose key-note I believe to be UNIVER-
SALIZATION, while the preceding great cycle ending around
100 B.C. had as basic key-note, CULTIVATION. But for
human beings who in various parts of the world are still totally bound to their natal soil and the field which their ancestors have cultivated for centuries -- and, even in the slums
of our cities, are likewise bound by ethnic characteristics,
or in a broader sense, can still flare up into nationalistic and
patriotic rages -- this process of universalization is only
beginning. Our theoretically Christian Western civilization provided men with mostly fanatic ideals and with com-

pelling urges for physical conquests and intellectual expansion which represent only the very first stage of this process of universalization. We have rushed forward, ever seeking more speed, more land to defoliate, more solid past to reduce to ashes. Now we are emerging from a kind of "solid state" of consciousness to a more "liquid" one.

Just as heat accelerates the motion of molecules, so modern technology has intensified the movements of human individuals and collectivities. We are reaching the Moon. It remains to be seen what this will do to mankind; but as I believe that the revolutions of the Moon around the earth define the boundaries of the earth's "aura" (or cosmo-magnetic field), all that we are able to do is to become aware of the occult extension of our humanity -- perhaps for the first time, though not necessarily so. We are reaching a point of vantage from which we can both see ourselves as one mankind living on one global home, the earth, and observe the universe free from the globe's atmosphere, free from the mirages produced by our geocentric and ego-conditioned minds.

This is only the beginning. We are moving from one level of consciousness to the next, from one level of "cultivation" to a more universalistic field of productivity which we will be able to make fruitful thanks to the new release of Aquarian powers. That too will only be one phase of the whole process of universalization. The next will open with the Capricorn-Cancer Age -- Phase Three of the great cyclic process of civilization -- and the following fourth phase, the Sagittarian-Gemini Age, should witness the concrete fulfillment on a perhaps much transformed Earth-surface of much of what the Aquarian Age enthusiasts expect quite miraculously to come "right now".

PART   THREE

What we know of the past of mankind's evolution should make it quite clear that one cannot separate history from geography and climate, nor mankind from the earth's biosphere. The succession of glacial Ages, the drying up of once fertile regions -- the deserts of Central Asia, for instance -- and the rise and fall (or drifting apart) of continents are basic, even if not too well known factors in this evolution. We know now that every kingdom of life, every oceanic and stratospheric current, and beyond these, the response of the ionosphere to "solar winds" or other electro-magnetic impacts -- which most likely follow some as yet undefined cyclic rhythm -- are closely inter-related. We are aware that geographical and climatic factors condition, and very likely determine, the fundamental characteristics of every local culture -- and all human cultures until now have been the expressions of local environmental conditions. The attachment of still the great majority of human beings to their birthland and to the social-cultural-religious traditions of their ancestors remains a powerfully binding factor, the importance of which is pathetically demonstrated today in the Arabic Near-East and in varying degrees everywhere on the globe.

In spite of this -- and, in the deepest meaning of this situation, b e c a u s e of this -- man has been told by the "great religions" now in existence that he is a "spiritual being" quite alien on this planet. He is brought to it, or created by God in it, to learn certain hard lessons and to fulfill a rather tragic part in the great Design of an omnipotent God Who has His being in a transcendent realm, man's only true "home". Somehow the whole earth and all it contains are made by this God for the sake of man's Soul, which nevertheless finds itself an exile on this planet.

This is not the place to discuss such ideas; they may be only a materialized and vulgarized version of profound metaphysical concepts. What is important for us here is to realize that these religious ideas have made very deep marks upon astrological thought as well as upon history, ethics, sociology and in general upon all that concerns the relationships between man and other living things in the biosphere, and now between man and the very soil, water and air of this planet. We act indeed as exiles or conquerors and plunderers of an alien land; and we have not yet quite abandoned a quasi-mystical approach to the capitalized word, History. We forget that without the earth there would be no mankind, and without continents and specific climatic regions, there would not be the variety of human peoples and cultures.

Today "ecology" has become a fashionable word; and there is even much recent talk concerning "cosmecology", the study of the relationship between man and his cosmic environment. We are told that a human being should no longer be seen as an isolated individual but as an individual-in-his-environment. But the crucial step, psychologically and even spiritually speaking, seems very hard to take for the immense majority of modern people, i. e. the step which would make us accept the fact that mankind plays a functional part within the "being" -- or the organized field of activity -- of the planet, Earth, perhaps just as the cerebro-spinal nervous system plays a functional part within the body of a human being.

The collective realization by all human beings that this Earth is a planetary whole, all the constituent parts of which (animate or supposedly inanimate, conscious or supposedly unconscious) have a definite quasi-organic function, has at long last been made possible by the work of geo-physicists and the daring circum-global travels of astronauts. Still more important, the presentation on T. V. screens of the image of our globe as an entity external to the photographers has made the earth as concrete and objectively real a fact of existence and consciousness as a traveler's home is when seen from a speeding train or a plane flying overhead. The fiery re-entry of the astronaut into this global "home" of mankind, as well as the tremendous consumption of energy needed to lift the space-traveling capsule from the threshold of this home, should illustrate how powerfully we are attached to our globe. We may leave it -- this is our privilege as thinking men. But so can the mind of an individual thinker leave, as it were (and perhaps literally so), the body within which it has developed and acquired structural consistency, and function outside of this body as an independent entity.

I believe that this reintegration of man into the quasi-organic "body" of the earth is perhaps the most important fact of our time. It occurs at the threshold of the Aquarian Age, because the basic premise of human consciousness in that Age should be not only the unity of all mankind, but the quasi-organicity of the earth and our united function (as united mankind, or Man) in this earth-Field -- which, I repeat, may in reality expand up to the moon. In ancient time, before the rise of transcendent religious philosophies, the earth was considered apparently to be the microcosm of the universe; then the cosmological picture changed under the pressure of the tide of individualization of consciousness within ego-structures, and the individual came to be seen as the microcosm of the universal macrocosm. Now the two conceptions should become integrated, the individual person remaining still a microcosm, but one that is operating collectively in the fulfillment of a definite function within the fields of ever larger planetary, solar-systemic and galactic wholes.

In other words, we should realize that there is a collective operation of Man-as-a-whole; and that this operation exists at several levels. The biosphere is the root-level at which mankind operates -- until now in a f r a g m e n t e d local-culture manner, but perhaps from now on in a g l o b a l l y i n t e r r e l a t e d way. Then there is the "noosphere" popularized recently by Teilhard de Chardin and representing at the level of the mind the growing unity of Man's psychism and the results of more hidden ("occult") interconnections and rhythmic interplays between races and cultures. And an ever increasing number of individuals are becoming aware, dimly and confusedly though it be, of a still more inclusive and subtle level of planetary existence and consciousness which Sri Aurobindo in India called "supermental", and to which H. P. Blavatsky referred a century ago as "the White Lodge". We might call it the t h e o s p h e r e .

ZODIACAL MAN AND
GEODETIC EQUIVALENTS

If I bring out such matters here, it is because it is essential for us to put in its true perspective the concept of the "Heavenly Man" which has played a very important part in astrology. Everyone who has read even the most popular astrology writings should be aware of the astrological connection which is generally made between the signs of the zodiac and the various parts of the human body. Aries is said to "rule" the head; Taurus, the neck; Gemini, the shoulders, arms and lungs; Cancer, the stomach and some phases of metabolism; Leo, the heart and the spine; Virgo, the upper abdomen with the liver, pancreas and small intestines; Libra, the kidney region; Scorpio, the large intestines and generative organs; Sagittarius, the thighs and sciatic nerves; Capricorn, the knees and the process of forward movement; Aquarius, the legs; Pisces, the feet.

Figures have been printed in which we see a man bent backward in a circle, and inscribed in a circle divided into zodiacal signs. On the other hand, we find in the Kabbalist tradition mention of the Great Heavenly Man, to whom various holy names are given, Whose body extends over the constellations. Here again we can see the confusion between the signs and the constellations of the zodiac. The idea that man was "made in the image of God" is a rather naive religious idea related to the concept of a personal God Who is the Heavenly Father with Whom man can hold a reassuring "dialogue". It may be largely a Hebraic concept, because the Hindu doctrine of Avatars featured in the Bhagavat Gita is actually quite different and closer to the Christian concept of an incarnation of God when philosophically or occultly understood.

If God is envisioned as Cosmic Man, such a majestic divine Form should be understood as the inner structure of the entire cosmos; galaxies may be considered as cells and single stars as atoms of this divine Body. What can be logically deduced from this anthropomorphic picture is that wherever there are planets inhabited by intelligent beings, these beings are also "sons" of the Cosmic Being and also made in His image -- so that we can expect to find people very much like us if we ever come in contact with such "space brothers".

On the other hand, when we establish correspondences between Aries, Taurus, etc. and sections of the human body we do not need to assume such a cosmic picture, because what we are referring to may be simply a correspondence between the twelve seasonal phases of the Sun-Earth relationship throughout the year (i.e. the signs of the zodiac) and these sections of the body. A zodiacal sign refers to one of twelve basic modes of solar energy. The tropical zodiac of signs measures the quality or character of solar energy striking the earth on any day of the year, and (symbolically at least) being distributed by the moon from new moon to new moon -- i.e. through a complete lunation cycle, of which there are (archetypally, but not exactly) twelve during an entire year. The fact that there are twelve such lunations during the year may very well have been the experiential foundation for dividing the "yearly path of the sun" into twelve zodiacal signs of thirty degrees each -- there being thirty days in a lunation cycle.

Why a corresponding division of the human body into the twelve regions above-mentioned has turned out to be valid insofar as astrological practice is concerned, this of course is a difficult question to answer. It may seem that too little importance is given to the winter signs of the zodiac; but then during winter the life-forces are more or less dormant. Vital energies are within the seed or the roots, and the human legs and feet might be considered symbolically as the roots of the human "tree" -- a tree which, however, can walk. Indeed this human walk is a most characteristic symbol of the human kingdom of life -- which may be why the Zen master, asked to define Zen, answered "Walk on!"; and why the ancient symbolic picture of "walking with God" (or with the Master) is found in many religious traditions.

Whatever was the manner in which the bio-zodiacal concepts originated, I firmly believe that these correspondences between Aries, Taurus, Gemini, etc. and twelve regions of the human body have nothing to do with constellations of stars. They deal with twelve centers of vital energies (prana, we might say) in the human body, centers normally vitalized successively through the year during twelve basic phases of the relationship between the sun and the earth -- which phases are represented by the twelve signs of the zodiac.

This has to be well understood by the reader in order that he or she be able to grasp the meaning of what is now to follow; that is, of attempts that have been made to project the zodiac upon the earth-globe, thus dividing the latter into twelve geodetic zones.

But which zodiac? That of constellations, or that of zodiacal signs?

To project the twelve sections of the zodiac upon the

earth's surface can only be done significantly if one can find valid reasons to make any particular 30-degree section of celestial (or orbital) space correspond to a particular 30-degree zone of terrestrial longitude. In other words where do we start? Where, for instance, does Aries 0° fall in terms of terrestrial longitude?

Here we have at the geographical level the same problem we had at the historical level; i. e. on what year does a nearly 26,000 year long cycle of precession of the equinoxes begin? In a very real sense, it is an insoluble problem. There have been dozens of dates given, both in India (where indeed there is not only one school of astrology) and in the modern Western world; likewise there have been, this century, at least three attempts to relate zodiacal longitudes to geographical longitudes, and here I am presenting a fourth one based on somewhat different premises and facts of observations at the geographical level. The Ptolemaic theory of astrological rulership of countries constitutes also an archaic attempt to relate zodiacal signs and earth-regions.

In an article printed in "American Astrology" (May 1945) a well-known astrologer and teacher, Ellen McCaffery wrote: "Ptolemy divided the whole world into four quarters. He took the 37th degree East Longitude as the meridian which in his time roughly separated Europe from Asia. This line runs through Aleppo which is 37 degrees East longitude, and almost through Moscow, which is $37\frac{1}{2}$ degrees East. He then took the latitude of 36 degrees north, from Gibralter, through the Mediterranean Sea along to Aleppo, which is 36 degrees 10 minutes north latitude. From these two lines he made a cross into which he divided the known world of his day into four parts, giving the three fire signs, Aries, Leo and Sagittarius, to the northwestern segment, the three air signs to the northeastern segment, the three water signs to the southwestern segment, and the three earth signs to the southeastern segment. Thus Europe was generally under the fire signs, northern Asia under the air signs, Africa under the water signs and southern Asia under the earth signs."

Mrs. McCaffery comments further that since Ptolemy's time vast changes in population and the confused development of modern nations have made it quite impossible to determine on that Ptolemaic basis any really valid correspondence between nations and zodiacal signs. But she seems to have accepted the system which the noted English astrologer, Sepharial, made popular, and which many astrologers are today taking for granted without really questioning its theoretical relevance.

In his "Theory of Geodetic Equivalents" Sepharial assumed to be correct what of course is the most simple, most obvious and most likely to become a popular solution of the problem. We count geographical longitude from Greenwich; therefore why not say that this 0-degrees of geographical longitude also refers to 0-degrees of celestial longitude -- to Aries 0°. Then the earth-zone between 0-degrees and 30-degrees geographical longitude e a s t would correspond to the whole sign of Aries -- the zone from geographical longitude 30-degrees to 60-degrees to the sign Taurus, etc. The zone extending from 0° longitude to 30° longitude w e s t corresponds to Pisces; from 30° to 60° to Aquarius; from 60° to 90°, to Capricorn (this includes all the eastern states of the U.S.A.); from 90° to 120°, to Sagittarius (most of western U.S.A., through San Francisco and all the coast north would come under Scorpio, and Alaska under Libra and Virgo).

I repeat that this is so simple a solution as to be easily acceptable without any thinking. But why should London be taken as the King-pin in the scheme? This may be a natural thing to do for an Englishman, as a deeply engrained sense of world-leadership has been built into the English mentality; but while we still retain the Greenwich meridian as a traditional starting point for geographical measurements, England's world-position today makes the selection less and less obvious. I can see actually no geographical reason for stating that the first longitude-zone of 30 degrees east of Greenwich corresponds to Aries any more than to any other sign; and without any such reason I find it hard personally to accept it, just as I cannot accept various dates given for the beginning of the "Piscean Age" without adequate historical reasons.

Can one find valid, or at least convincing geographical reasons to correlate a longitude-zone or degree of longitude with any particular region or locality on the surface of the globe?

Some authors have felt they could, and the locality selected has been the Great Pyramid in Egypt -- which, according to their calculations, stands at the center of the land area of the globe and, according to a persistent occult tradition, was built by very ancient pre-Egyptian races, not as a tomb, but as a place of Initiation. This Great Pyramid (not the others) is supposed to be a monument built according to really cosmic proportions, and in a sense as a "meeting place" between Heaven and Earth. It is said to have been built a whole precessional cycle before the date usually given by modern Egyptologists.

I personally believe in this old tradition which has been stressed not only by H. P. Blavatsky, but by several independent researchers and archaeologists, including an old Bahai friend of mine, Dr. Getzinger, who claimed that he had proofs that the base of the Pyramid had been washed several times by the sea. The most noted student of the Pyramid was, late last century, Albert Ross Parsons who wrote a book "The Great Pyramid: Its Divine Message", which has had a lasting influence on many serious minds, even if it has been used by less perspicacious and sound persons to back up various theories and "prophecies". What Mr. Parsons did, however, was to spread the constellations of stars -- and not only the zodiacal ones -- all over the globe. He spread the celestial map of stars over a planispheric map of the earth, using as an "anchorage" the Great Pyramid (that is, east longitude $31^{o}08'$ and north latitude $29^{o}59'$). One needs such an anchorage, for the earth-globe is constantly rotating around its polar axis, and thus there is no reason why one should, as it were, stop the globe at one point and then project the star-contents of the sky upon its surface. For various reasons dealing with Pyramidal and occult data, the locality of the Pyramid was made to correspond to the middle point in the c o n s t e l l a t i o n Taurus.

Some fifty years later, an American astrologer, who wrote books and articles for the magazine "American Astrology", Edward Johndro, while retaining the basic concept of Parsons, came to believe that the correlation between the zodiac and the earth-globe was not a static one, because of the fact of the precession of the equinoxes. In other words, at one time certain regions of the globe correspond to, or are "ruled" by mid-Taurus; but the same regions 2160 years later correspond to mid-Gemini -- for the whole zodiac has been moving w e s t w a r d. According to Mr. Johndro, 0° Aries corresponded around 1930 to $29^{o}10'$ of geographical longitude west, and that first degree of the zodiac was moving westward at the precessional rate of 72 years per degree of longitude.

Another American astrologer, Paul Council, followed the same trend of ideas; but, though using the Great Pyramid as starting point, he came for various reasons, mainly related to the position of the star Aldebaran at a certain time, to assign around 1930 another geographical value to Aries 0°, i. e. west geographical longitude $36^{o}42'$.

In order to evaluate the significance of such theories one has to realize that two different sets of factors are actually being considered. If this is not clear, confusion is bound to reign. Albert Parsons' system of correspondence between the Sky-macrocosm and the Earth-microcosm was based on the old Hermetic (and indeed Chinese) cosmology, which has been succinctly formulated in the statement: As above, so below. The entire Chinese system of life was based on the concept that the order of the Sky had to be precipitated upon the chaotic earth-surface (or, socially speaking, the State) through the intermediary of a kind of focusing agent, the Emperor.

Such a type of thinking can be found everywhere, more or less developed, at the level of tribal organization -- even when the tribe has become expanded into some kind of kingdom under a more or less theocratic system. It was strongly in evidence in Egypt, and we find it operating on a smaller scale in Black African cultures (in the region of the Sudan, for instance) as well as in the American Indian pueblos of New Mexico and Arizona. At such a stage of cultural and religious development one finds a deeply rooted belief that in the kingdom or the pueblo there is a sacred spot at which either a special connection between the Sky-gods and the kingdom is focused, or one can find the entrance to a secret path which leads to the center of the earth.

The old tradition is that the Great Pyramid was such a sacred place, a link between the celestial and the earthly realms. It was therefore the place at which sacred Initiations were performed. It was, in this sense at least, the "center" of the earth-surface, of Man's world. Through it, as through an engine, the energies of the cosmos were released upon this world. For the old Egyptians, Egypt was of course the central reality of Man's world -- and so was China for the Chinese, India (the old Aryavarta) to the Hindus, Rome to the Romans. To the French people with roots in the past, Paris is la Ville-Lumiere (the City that is Light); and to the English claiming a special world-wide mission for sacred Albion, it is indeed logical to have geographical measurements keyed to the Greenwich meridian.

It would seem, however, that the pragmatic and practical English astrologer based his theory on the zodiac of signs, not on an attempt to discover which place on Earth corresponded to what celestial fixed star; or at least the astrologers who use his system in what is often called "location astrology" are concerned with the correspondence between geographical longitudes and celestial right ascension -- right ascension being measured on the equatorial plane and not too different from celestial longitude, measured along the ecliptic. For instance, if the conjunction of Jupiter and Uranus occurs at the right ascension corresponding to Libra 2^O (or celestial longitude 182°), then the "influence" of this conjunction may be said to be focused upon regions located at the 178° longitude west (some of the Aleutian Islands, Midway Island, etc.) because the sign Libra extends from 180° to 150° west longitude, as Libra 0° corresponds to the International Date Line in mid-Pacific and the degrees of zodiacal longitude always progress westward on the globe. And I should add here that if one wants to make a "location chart" for any city, what the "geodetic equivalent" refers to is the Mid-Heaven of the place. The locality's Ascendant must be found in an ordinary Table of Houses for the geographical latitude of the city.

The practical value of the system is quite obvious. If the Mid-Heaven and Ascendant of a person's birth-place do not fit well with this person's birth-planets, he may find life more harmonious and easy in another geographical location; and if an "unfortunate" planetary conjunction hits the meridian or Ascendant of the place at which the individual resides, and also affects his own chart, he may palliate greatly the unfortunate "influence" by moving to some other locality. He can in fact, in a sense, modify his own birth-chart by moving to another longitude and latitude.

Such at least is the rather popular belief in some astrological circles where the validity of Sepharial's system is not even questioned; and according to many people "it works". Perhaps it does to some extent, at this time and for people of our Western world, for the same reason that the English language may conceivably be accepted as an international language; but, every consistent astrological system seems to work for the astrologers who are thoroughly familiar with it and fully believe in its value. This is why I have always stated that astrology is a symbolic language and not an exact empirical science.

If the correspondence between celestial and geographical longitudes is to be considered as set once-for-all, and thus as a fact of Nature, then the tropical zodiac of signs would be considered the "fixed" factor in astrology -- and not the sidereal zodiac of constellations. In this sense, the theory of geodetic equivalents, as commonly used, seems to confirm the position I have taken throughout this book. The great stars move over the face of the Earth. Their passages over the Mid-Heavens of geographical localities could be indeed very significant in terms of telluric changes. But again I must repeat, I can see no absolutely valid reason, besides convenience and ease of calculation, for saying that a star like Betelgeuze having Gemini 28°15 for its zodiacal longitude is therefore focusing its rays or influence upon geographical longitude 88°15' west, that is, at the longitude of Eastern Siberia, Sinkiang, central Tibet, Darjeeling (India) and the Indian Ocean -- though, of course, the correlation between the star and that meridian may be important, as possibly some great personage connected with the beginning of the New Age may be born and live in such a zone of longitude.

If one correlates as a permanent fact the twelve s i g n s of the zodiac measured on the ecliptic with twelve 30-degree sections of geographical longitude, what one does, I repeat, is to relate symbolically each of the twelve sections of the big orange, the earth-globe, with the twelve monthly phases of the vital relationship between the earth and the sun. One establishes thus twelve vitality-zones on the globe, each zone having possibly a focalizing geographical point or region -- just as the human body is said to have six great c h a k r a s (or magnetic vortices of energy) and a semi-transcendent one on the top of the head, which could correspond to the

North Pole region (the point of reception for certain solar or cosmic energies, according to the occult tradition). Indeed one could say that the zodiacal circle (ecliptic) is actually divided into six "male-female" sections, Aries-Taurus, Gemini-Cancer, etc.; and so would the earth-globe be divided, each of the six geographical zones having a particular significance in terms of the distribution of solar-cosmic electro-magnetism throughout the biosphere.

If this be clearly understood, the question then can be asked: Are there any geographical indications which could give us a clue as to the most significant way of interpreting the nature of these geographical longitude-zones -- and of changes constantly occurring in these zones -- by correlating them with astrological signs of the zodiac, and with the cyclic motions of the planets and the stars in the sky?

In other words, what we want to try to establish now is a kind of world-chart with six or twelve "houses" -- an at least relatively permanent chart, within the framework of which one could plot the series of changes taking place in the cosmic "ambient" of the Earth, the solar system and (eventually) the galaxy.

How can we go about doing it, if we do not care to accept Greenwich as a fundamentally significant base, just because of a perhaps obsolescent European tradition? We must see a new kind of procedure, a realistic ·approach to the morphology of the earth-surface.

THE GEOMORPHIC APPROACH

In 1945-46 I wrote a book (long out of print) which its New York publisher, the Philosophical Library, insisted on printing under the inadequate title "Modern Man's Conflicts: The Creative Challenge of a Global Civilization". The sub-title was allright, but the title will be, when republished, "Harmony Through Conflicts".

In the second Part of the book there is a chapter entitled "The Road to Global Harmony"; and I would like to quote at length from the sub-section "Elements of Global Morphology", for the facts stated in it and the interpretation of these facts are the foundation for the system of geo-zodiacal correspondences I shall be presenting.

"Let us look at the earth-globe. We should have learned to see it as a globe pivoting around the polar axis; its continental masses of land and oceans dotted with islands, big and small, spreading over its surface in characteristic shapes. Here mankind lives. Within this global field men produce and strive to reach harmony within themselves and with one another -- strive, alas, so far most unsuccessfully as a rule. How can they hope to reach harmony as men, if they do not understand the harmony that chords all lands and seas as a dynamic whole, as an integral field of operation? The earth-surface is a whole, and it is dynamic in as much as it is constantly in motion and in a state of morphological change. The earth whirls in space in a complex combination of motions which constantly modify the 'geomorphic' and geostatic equilibrium of its lands, seas and air-currents. Mountains and continents rise and fall. Ice ages come in waves. There may be even greater changes in the polarization and axial inclination of our globe as a whole, whence vast cataclysms that imprint deep-seated remembrances in the collective unconscious of all civilizations.

"The earth may not be strictly speaking 'alive'; but it is the matrix -- or matricial field -- from which all living organisms emerge and within which they operate in unity or diversity, as material organisms and as participants in a cosmic-planetary drama of evolution. Most living organisms remain unconscious of this participation, live and die in a, to them, meaningless sequence. A few human beings at all times reach full and direct consciousness of this great evolution; give to their less aware comrades visions and symbols to foreshadow what the latter in turn may come to experience; and, passing on, remain as indivisible units of consciousness and power within the great oneness of Man.

"From the thin layers of this earth-surface, all life springs forth. Surely, if we can only visualize and understand our global world as a whole of organically (or quasi-organically) inter-related parts and functions, we may end by sensing and perhaps clearly understanding what each of these continental and oceanic parts represents in the economy of the whole. What we need is a sense of gestalt -- that is, of integral form -- and of symbolic values; to which the records of history (and even of persistent world-wide traditions) should add much meaning, if they too are understood in terms of 'wholes of time', i. e. of cycles. We need a new approach to geography and to the geographical basis of history and civilization; we need, both, an integrative approach and an engineer's approach -- thus we need branches of knowledge which we have called respectively 'geomorphics' and 'geotechnics'.

"Our planet is a whole; human civilization is a whole. In the Age of plenitude, of which we speak throughout this book, creative fulfillment can only come to man as these wholes are taken as foundations for living, feeling and thinking. What we named 'geotechnics' is the science of management of the total resources of the earth as an all-inclusive field of operation. And by geomorphics' we mean the understanding of the structure of this field, not primarily in terms of the amount of materials, energy and human beings available for production on each and all lands or seas, but rather in terms of the geomorphic structure and shape of continents and oceans. These global structures, after all, condition climates and population, migrations and the course of civilization. They are as significant to anyone attempting to understand the past, present and future of humanity as a whole, as the study of the shape of a person's body and features is to the endocrinologist and psychologist (or even criminologist) whose business it is to understand the temperament, character and behavior of men. We might thus speak of geo-

morphics as a kind of geognomy similar in intent to phys-
iognomy; a modern and scientific version of the latter having been provided by Dr. Sheldon's studies in "The Varieties
of Human Physique" (Harper, 1940) and his classification of
human bodies and temperaments into viscerotonic, somato-
tonic, and cerebrotonic.

"I can only briefly suggest here the possibilities of this
new field of geomorphic study, but a typical instance can be
pointed out which will lead us to the main point of this chapter. This instance is the remarkable morphologic similarity between Asia and Europe. Both Asia and Europe have
three southward peninsulas. Indo-China, India and Arabia
match respectively Greece, Italy and Spain. Ceylon is the
structural equivalent of Sicily; Indonesia, of Crete and the
Greek Archipelago down to Rhodes (which is, in a very general sense, a miniature Australia).

"If we look at the continental mainland, we find Tibet (and
the adjacent mountain ranges of China) matching Switzerland
and Bohemia. The Mongolian and Siberian plains correspond to Germany and Poland, China in the East is like European Russia; while in the West, central France stands for
Persia, with Brittany, like Syria and Palestine -- the Gir-
onde and Dordogne valleys with their prehistoric cultures
paralleling that of the Tigris and Euphrates.

"Such correspondences might seem mere chance figura-
tions were it not that there is a startling parallelism between
the characteristics of the cultures which have developed in
these corresponding geographical structures. Indo-China
with her highly developed art and music, and Java with her
rich culture, remind one forcibly of Greece and the earlier
Cretan civilizations. India has been the center of religious
doctrines for Asia, just as Italy has been for Europe. The
ancient city of Nasik, sacred to Rama, stands (near Bombay)
where Rome is in Italy; Benares, where Florence grew. Cur-
iously enough the Arabs settled in Spain (Arabia's structural
equivalent in Europe), and both Arabia and Spain are rugged

lands, angular shaped, with fanatic, intense, proud popula-
tions. As significant are the historical-cultural correspondences between the nations which grew respectively in Persia and in France (Zoroastrian civilization matching the old
Celtic culture), in Mongolia and in Germany (military and
mystical peoples avid for space-conquest in an inorganic
sense), in China and Russia (lands of the 'good earth' and of
robust peasantry long controlled by a small aristocracy).

"The general picture presented by the relationship of Europe to Asia is that of miniature to full-sized original. Europe is not unlike the budding protuberance on a navel orange,
which is a small replica of the orange itself. It appears thus
as a specialized reproduction of the vast Motherland for a
particular evolutionary purpose. In another sense, of real
historical-cultural validity, we might say that Europe is to
Asia as the conscious and intellectual part of man's total
psyche is to the vast collective unconscious. The conscious
is a differentiated organ of the unconscious, in the sense that
the brain and the cerebrospinal nervous system constitute
differentiated organs of the total human organism. Religion
is the progeny of the collective unconscious (Asia); science,
that of the rational conscious (Europe).

"In such a parallelism differences are as significant as
similarities. We spoke of Italy and India, Switzerland and
Tibet as occupying similar places in the two geomorphic
structures. But we should notice at once the fact that the
Alps describe a convex arc of mountains above the Northern
Italian plains, while the Himalayas describe a concave arc
over the plains of Northern India. If we consider the two
mountainous masses of Switzerland and Tibet as the 'geo-
spiritual' centers of their respective continents, we get the
idea of the European center radiating outward, while the Asiatic center is focused inward; and we see how well this describes the difference between the European and Asiatic type
of spirituality.

"Another way of looking at the Eurasian land-mass is to

see it as one shape extending from 10° longitude west (West Ireland) to 170° longitude west (Eastern tip of Siberia). Dividing into two this span of 200 degrees of longitude, we find longitude 90° east as the pivotal meridian; and it passes through Calcutta, Tibet, near Lhassa and near the highest mountain of the golbe, just west of the Gobi Desert and the Mongolian People's Republic, through a most important part of Siberia (Sibirsk region) and along the great Ienisei river which may become a great trade-route in the future. Around the pivot of this 90° east meridian we might see soon the total population of the Eurasian world almost evenly divided; even now the combined population of India, Persia and the U.S.S.R. balance approximately that of China, Japan, Indo-China and Indonesia. And there is a general similarity of position between the Scandinavian peninsula and Kamchatka, the British Isles and Japan -- the correlation between the last two island-groups being particularly significant in terms of world-history and racial background.

"The main point we wish to make here, however, is the polar relationship between, on one hand, the big land mass constituted by Europe, Asia and Africa (or 'Eurasiafrica') and on the other, the Americas. This relationship provides the logical foundation for the future global society. It establishes the great geomorphic dualism of human civilization. Just as the North and South Pole regions are complementary in that the former is an apparently empty circle of water, while the latter is a quasi-circular land-mass; so the two basic continental structures of the earth, America and Eurasiafrica, have shapes whose characteristics complement and polarize each other.

"The Americas can be reduced in shape to two southward pointing triangles -- a symbol of 'descent' of spirit and 'masculine' activity; while Eurasiafrica is a sprawling 'feminine' shape, with Europe as a highly differentiated miniature form of the great mother of races and religions, Asia. Some geologists have claimed that at one time the two continental masses were united, then broke away very slowly (over many tens of thousands of years) -- the line of fission being now in the Atlantic ocean. The western contour of Europe-Africa and the eastern shores of the Americas suggest broadly such a possibility -- if the western bulge of Africa is made to fit into the depression of the Gulf of Mexico and the southern coast of the United States.

"We are inclined to believe that the mythical Atlantis might have been, rather than a now sunken continent, this whole continental mass before it broke in two; in other words, the earth's continents in a condition of undivided unity -- whereas now they constitute essentially two polarized masses. This would be significant if it could be proven true -- in that it would correlate with the mythological reference to an Atlantean humanity, at first pure and sinless, then dividing into two camps as a result of the abuse and misuse of sexual powers.

"However this may be, the fact is that today man's global field of operation is typically bi-polar. At the center of the two land-masses we find, in Eurasiafrica, the Mediterranean Sea and, in the Americas, the Gulf of Mexico. The former has been a focal point for Eurasiafrican culture; the latter has also been, and presumably will even more become, a focus for the Pan-American culture which, after a number of centuries (and perhaps even millennia) will gradually be established, we may well presume, as an entirely new human expression. Today 'American' civilization, North and South, is fundamentally an outgrowth of European impulses and ideologies; and we believe it is merely a matrix into which new spiritual seeds have been and are being sown, which will take a very long time to mature, through many crises and probable obscurations. It seems likely that the first typical developments in truly American culture will come from the lands surrounding the Gulf of Mexico -- Mexico itself being a probable focus, as it also was in the time of the Mayans, and perhaps long before.

"All of which may be called speculations, and must remain so until a new understanding of planetary cycles of geological and anthropological development is reached. What is factual and very concrete, however, is the relationship (historical, political and economic as well as geomorphic) between the Americas and Eurasiafrica -- and particularly today, while human civilization is still predominantly 'north-hemispheric', between North America (including what is unfortunately called Central America) and Eurasia. Global harmony and international peace depend almost entirely upon the type of relationship and interchange established between these two complementary masses of land and of humanity.

"We are not referring here to the Communist ideology or the political methods of the Soviets. We are speaking of concrete and realistic facts of geography and history, and of nothing else. Basically, it is these facts which determine, if not political systems and cultural ideals in themselves, at least their failure or success in establishing themselves on a particular soil. Likewise, the supremacy of England in world-politics was founded upon the fact that she, as an insular outpost of Europe to the west, was in position to use pre-eminently and to capitalize upon the gold and cotton of America, and to merchandize and transport across the seas much of America's wealth, especially after Spain's downfall. Now, however, that the Americas are becoming definitely established as one of the poles of a global economy, and that Soviet Russia has aroused to productive activity the central regions of Eurasia, the role of England is becoming unnecessary in terms of geotechnics -- even if it can be still considered very important in the realm of spiritual values and world-civilization; provided the English people can focus their creative energy there.

"The role of French culture can be similarly understood in terms of the fact that France links the Northern seas, the

Atlantic and the Mediterranean, and is the westernmost outlet of Eurasia -- more so than Spain, whose geotechnical significance resides in her position as the western point of contact between Africa and Europe, this fact having predestined her to be the seat of the great Mozarabic culture and thus a most important link between the Near East and France at a crucial time of European history (around 900 A.D.). France is, by her position, a natural outpost for the Russian hinterland of Europe, being the point of convergence of Northern, Central and Mediterranean Europe -- and as well of North Africa; and in as much as a passively polarized Africa responds to an active and positive Europe, France's control over West North Africa -- from Tunisia to the Congo, with Dakar as a center -- was an inevitable geotechnical result. For the same reason, Russia is bound, sooner or later, to expand her influence over Egypt and the Arab world (written in 1946!), England's hegemony there being a transitional factor which must lose its basic importance as a global polarization becomes fully established between the U.S.S.R. and the U.S.A.

"Triangular North America and crescent-shape Eurasia are today as man and woman in the great ritual of full global production; and much of what we have written concerning the relationship between man and woman as consciously productive polarities could apply basically to what the relation between U.S.A. and U.S.S.R. should be. But it never can be a creative relationship in terms of physical and spiritual abundance until the American people come to discover and fully accept their world-destiny as releasers of a new civilizing spirit -- a new logos. Which means, first of all, until the American people overcome their collective adolescent mother-complex, and American men come into their own as positive civilizing agents outside of the field of merely physical business productivity and management.

"What we are facing today is a new global birth of human

society, based on new (because untried) principles of human relationship. And the great symbol of this gradual emergence of a new world is the o n e   o c e a n,   m a t r i x   o f   t h e   o n e w o r l d. All birthing is out of some "sea". And as long as men could conceive only of separate seas with distinguishing names, or at best of "the seven seas", it was impossible for the "one world" to be born. But now, thanks to our global and total war, men have come to consider all seas as one ocean, and to visualize the earth as a globe. In terms of this new geographical sense Soviet Russia and North America have become close neighbors w h o s e   b o d i e s   e n c i r c l e   t h e N o r t h   P o l e   a n d   i t s   s t a r -- a great and profound symbol, indeed!

"One ocean and, out of it, two vast continental masses fanning out from the North Pole. Humanity speeds now through this one ocean and its atmospheric counterpart; breathes the one air which unites all individuals and nations, even the most proud isolationists; is nervously and visually stimulated by sounds and pictures which fill the radio strata with the chaos and the yearnings of confused and insecure, but aspiring and aroused collectivities. As men travel swiftly from continent to continent, even a large continent can be seen as one huge island; and as men's minds listen to radio music and voices from many races and nations, and see on the screen people of various colors and features perform daily tasks conditioned by the common humanity of all, they gradually realize that all nations, large or small, are like islands of consciousness and culture emerged from the one ocean of man's generic and collective unconscious."

What I wrote nearly twenty-five years ago is as valid today as it was then. In spite of what has been happening since then in China, and of the more or less concerted rise of the "Third World", the basic fact remains, under all surface-storms of international politics: the polarization between the Americas and Eurasiafrica. However when the Egyptian

Great Pyramid was considered the center of the inhabitable world, the emphasis was placed on Eurasiafrica. The Nile delta occupied a very significant place within this vast landmass; and it seems quite likely -- though impossible to prove today by our available scientific means -- that a very ancient Egyptian civilization preceding our historical records was indeed directly related to the last island (Plato's Poseidonis) which is supposed to have disappeared under the Atlantic sea-surface around 8000 B.C.

The Great Pyramid was not built alone. It was linked by a passage way to the lower part of the mysterious Sphinx; and, though I cannot of course "prove" the validity of this statement, the Sphinx and the Pyramid constituted a meaningful ritualistic whole. The Sphinx towered over the entrance of the gateway marking the entrance of a passageway which symbolized the "Path of Initiation" -- and many other things besides. This passageway led to some perhaps as yet unobserved entrance to the Pyramid which, I repeat, was the sacred place of Initiation. The neophyte, after passing successfully through various testing ordeals, was put by the Initiator into a condition of trance for three days, during which he underwent further tests, experiences and a change of psychic polarity -- to arise, if successful, "after the third day" as an Initiate of the Great Mysteries. *

In the symbolism of the zodiac, I believe that while the Pyramid, as the place of Initiation, refers to Libra 0⁰**,

---

*Such a process has been described in various ways by various authors. I might refer particularly to Edward Schure "The Great Initiates", and to a more recent and quite fascinating book "Initiation" by Elizabeth Haich (Allen and Unwin Ltd., London, 1960) which is no doubt partly autobiographical.

**The fall equinox is, in a deep sense, the most "spiritual" moment of the year -- cf. the last chapter of my book "The Pulse of Life".

the Sphinx is a symbol of the transition between the signs
Leo and Virgo. This mythological creature has been interpreted in several ways; some authors have seen in it a symbolical composite of the "fixed signs", Leo, Scorpio and
Aquarius. This may be true of some sphinx-like entities,
like the one which was defeated by Oedipus; but the Egyptian
Sphinx does not belong to that category. It is simply a composite being which is half lion and half human virgin. It represents the cusp between Leo and Virgo; and that point of
the zodiac symbolizes the struggle which man has to face as
he decides to "enter the Path" that will lead him, if successful, to a new level of consciousness and a new type of life
dedicated to humanity-as-a-whole (the "Great Orphan", symbolically speaking).

At the Leo-Virgo cusp man must accept the fact that he
has now to learn to overcome his fierce pride, his sense of
ego-centered isolation and his resulting love for self-dram-
atization -- and to become a "Servant" of humanity as well
as of his god-like inner selfhood. This gradual acceptance,
which means a total repolarization of his nature and his consciousness comes only after having passed through many
tests and crises; and this difficult process is represented in
zodiacal symbolism by the sign, Virgo. Now, Virgo, according to the traditional correspondence between zodiacal
signs and parts of the human body, represents the region of
the solar plexus and the organs of metabolism, the liver, the
pancreas, the duodenum and all the small intestines. Metabolism is a process of assimilation; and in Virgo, man
is symbolically assimilating the contents of his experiences
as an individualized person, and transmuting his responses to these experiences -- thus his emotional patterns,
the quality of his feeling-reactions to life, his complexes.

It is over this entire bio-chemical, bio-psychic and spiritual process that the Sphinx stands guard. The ancient name
for Egypt was Chem, from which we derived the term,
chemistry. Indeed the essential meaning of the Egyptian cul-

ture and the great secret of its Lodge of Initiates -- whose color was (and apparently still is) g r e e n -- is the process of meta-chemistry. It is most likely that the use of certain drugs was prevalent at least among some groups of seekers in later times; and perhaps in this (and the present use of L. S. D. and other psychedelic substances in America) we see a confirmation of the idea, advanced by the great Theosophist, William Q. Judge, that the present-day United States constitutes a cyclic reappearance of the ancient Egyptian people -- witness our practice of embalming corpses and many subtler correspondences, including a perhaps very significant link between Alexandria and New York.

However this may be, the meaning of the Sphinx is, in my opinion, a most important clue to a correspondence between signs of the zodiac and regions of the Earth-globe. If we say that the Sphinx stands at the g e o g r a p h i c a l longitude which corresponds to the degree of c e l e s t i a l longitude marking the transition between the zodiacal signs Leo and Virgo, we establish thereby a geo-celestial parallelism which throws a very fascinating light on the geomorphic significance of the shape and character of continents and countries.

THE EARTH AS AN ORGANIC WHOLE

By establishing correspondences between the signs of the zodiac and 30-degree longitude-bands at the surface of the globe, all I intend to say is that, as one considers the planet Earth as an organized system of interdependent activities (and perhaps as a "living" organism, if one gives to the term life, a broadly cosmic meaning), one can identify significantly the root-centers of this system of activities by using the zodiac of signs as a kind of "measuring rod". At the risk of repeating myself -- but repetitions are necessary where there is so much confusion -- I shall add that the tropical zodiac of signs refers to the relationship between the Sun (source of all vital energies) and the globe of the Earth --

and primarily to the Earth's biosphere. When we are projecting zodiacal signs upon this biosphere, we are therefore using these projected signs as means of defining six or twelve geographical regions, each of which should be dominated by some focusing center of energy -- one might say, by a planetary chakra.

Starting from the premise that the earth-location of the Sphinx and the Pyramid ($31^o07'57''$ east longitude and $29^o58'44''$ North latitude) corresponds to the cusp between the zodiacal signs, Leo and Virgo, we find that Leo 0° corresponds to east longitude $1^o08'$; Cancer 0° to west longitude $28^o52'$; Gemini 0° to west longitude $58^o52'$; Taurus 0° to west longitude $88^o52'$; Aries 0° to west longitude $118^o52'$.

Going eastward (following the direction of the globe's rotation around its axis), we find Libra 0° corresponding to east longitude $61^o08'$; Scorpio 0°, to east longitude $91^o08'$; Sagittarius 0°, to east longitude $121^o08'$, etc. The International Date Line in mid-Pacific at east longitude 180° would therefore correspond very closely to the Capricorn-Aquarius cusp; i. e. it would fall at $1^o08'$ Aquarius.

Let us briefly study these longitude zones beginning with east longitude $121^o08'$ and proceeding westward.

SCORPIO ZONE: from $121^o08'$ to $91^o08'$. This region includes China and Mongolia, the Siberian Lake Baikal county (which has been said by some travellers to have a very magical, occult atmosphere); and to the south, Indo-China and Indonesia. This is the cradle-land of the yellow races, which I believe are "ruled" by Scorpio insofar as their physical organisms and root-nature are concerned. The great Mongolian invasions which unfurled upon Europe during the Christian era were presumably launched from such a region. We might add that as Neptune is passing through the zodiacal sign Scorpio, one of the main spotlights in world-affairs -- perhaps the most vital -- has been focused upon Mao Tse Tung's arousal of the Chinese youth and upon the war in Viet Nam, also upon the anti-Communist power-struggle in Java.

The Libra-Scorpio cusp falls just at the capital of Tibet, Lhassa at geographical east longitude 91°11'; and if anything is Scorpionic in nature it certainly is, or was, the Tibetan social system, so deeply influenced by Tantric procedures and occult magic. The mysterious Gobi desert is included in this Scorpio zone; and the occult invisible city, Shamballah, is supposed to be located there.

LIBRA ZONE: from 91°08' to 61°08'. This zone encompasses the whole of India and Ceylon, Western Tibet, and an important section of Siberia, cut from north to south by the river, Yenisei, one of the world's largest. It seems most fitting to see greater India (the ancient Aryavarta) in such a Libra zone, which includes also the eastern part of Persia, Turkestan and the Ural mountains region -- a vital part of Soviet Russia. It was thanks to the industrial activities of this region that Russia was able to defeat the Nazi armies. The important cities of Sverdlovsk and Magnetovorsk (60°38') mark the beginning of this 30-degree zone of longitude, while Calcutta, India, is located at 88°20'. Calcutta dominates the Bengal region from which the philosophy and practices of the Tantra seem to have originated, at least with reference to what we know today of this approach to life.

If we consider Libra and Scorpio as two poles "male-female" aspects of one zodiacal unit, we see that this dyad includes by far the larger part of Asia, from the Urals to Peking, China. It stands at the geographical polar opposite (the antipodes) of most of North America -- that is, of the continental region bordered, on the one hand by Los Angeles, California, and Labrador in Eastern Canada. Lhassa in Tibet is at the antipodes of St. Louis. The Mountain States of the United States, centering at about 112° (Grand Canyon, Arizona) are located at the antipodes of Benares and the Himalayas.

In the Sepharial scheme of "geodetic equivalents" most

of India and Tibet would be located in the Cancer zone, and the whole of the American Mid-West in the Capricorn zone. This does not seem too adequate a correlation, while relating this American Mid-West to Taurus, symbol of fruitfulness and productivity certainly makes much sense.

VIRGO ZONE: from 61°08' to 31°08. This includes all that we usually call the Near-East, i.e. Palestine, Arabia, Mesopotamia, Persia, Turkey, most of European Russia, and to the south the Eastern coast of Africa, including its high mountains and the island of Madagascar. Historians once thought that agriculture and civilization had originated in the valleys south of the Caucasus -- and we still speak of the Caucasian races -- but now the new vogue is to trace the origin of man to the south-eastern sectio of Africa -- still in the same Virgo longitude zone. The Zoroastrian, Egyptian (Akh-na-ton), Mosaic, Christian, Islamic and Bahai religions had their origin in that same region of the globe, between North latitudes 25° and 35°. This fits well the Virgo character, for all such so-called "higher religions" represent various ways for man to reach and to serve a personalized God, Who is seen as the Exemplar and Teacher; i.e. they involve a personal relationship of devoted service (Virgo) between man (in the midst of a crisis of self-transformation) and God.

At a different level, modern Communist Russia emphasizes work and the laboring class, as well as an intellectual approach worshipful of a type of science, to which we may well attribute a typically Virgo (i.e. analytical) character -- for instance, Pavlov's experiments. It is also perhaps typical of Virgo (symbol of the "critical state" between the different levels of material organization) to stress the need for revolutionary activity and as well the longing for one kind or another of idealized Millennium.

The conjunctions of Uranus and Pluto in the sign, Virgo, could be said to have stirred up, or "clocked" the Arab-Israel conflict.

LEO ZONE: from 31°08' to 1°08'. This section of the globe encompasses the whole of central and western Europe, as well as most of Africa, from Algeria to South Africa. Leo is certainly an adequate symbol for this Western Europe which has arrogated herself the right to dominate and control the whole Earth. Leo represents the human ego and its urge for self-expression and conquest. Here we have witnessed the activities of nations claiming to be "master races" from ancient Rome to modern England and Germany. Paris, Ville lumiere where once le Roi Soleil (the Sun-King, Louis XIV) ruled, is the cusp city of this zone of the globe, at 2°20' east longitude. On the other side of the cusp -- the end of the Cancer zone -- stands London, and most of England, ruler of the seven seas (Cancer is a water sign).

CANCER ZONE: from 1°08' east to 28°52' west longitude. England, Ireland, the western part of France, Spain and Portugal and West Africa are found in that zone -- and much of the Atlantic Ocean, including Iceland. We find there some of the great sea-faring people. The strategic Azores Islands are just at the Gemini-Cancer cusp.

GEMINI ZONE: from 28°52' to 58°52' west longitude. In the northern region we have Greenland, and below the equator, Brazil, whose westernmost towns are located within the 35th degree of longitude. We do not know yet what will emerge of this vast country; but it is likely to have a very important future in the centuries ahead -- perhaps because there will be much destruction in the northern hemisphere.

TAURUS ZONE: from 58°52' to 88°52'. This includes the whole of western South America and the Atlantic coast of North America -- and we often fail to realize that the furthest western point in South America and the Panama Can-al are at about 80° west longitude, which is the longitude of Palm Beach in Florida, Charleston in Virginia and Harrisburg in Pennsylvania. This zone ends just east of St. Louis and New Orleans and west of Chicago. It includes all of Central America, Cuba and the Gulf of Mexico. It therefore refers to the Maya, Aztec, etc. cultures of Mexico. Interestingly, the shape of the gulf of Mexico region suggests that of a cross-section of the throat, with Florida as the epiglotis; Yucatan, prolonged by Cuba and the Antilles, could be considered as a tongue. There may be food for thought in such a morphological "Signature", in so far as Mexican culture is concerned.

ARIES ZONE: from $88^O52'$ to $118^O52'$. Within this zone we find mainly the Mountain States and Southern California, including the Los Angeles region (longitude $118^O15'$). Santa Barbara (longitude $119^O42'$) is just at the eastern end of the Pisces zone. Reno is on the Western border of the Aries zone. This region, thus, can be related to the head of the zodiacal Man, just as western Europe is to be related to his heart-center, and the Near-East to the solar plexus. If this seems strange, let us not forget that "form follows function" as architects often say; and that we are dealing here with potentialities of collective human development. Above all, we should not identify head with the cerebral cortex and intellectual thought. There are many other organic centers within the cranium than the organ of human intelligence, the fore-brain -- some of which refer to the capacity for vision and image-making. Indeed Hollywood has produced "images" which have circulated through and influenced the whole of mankind.

Besides, we should consider the Aries and Taurus zone as a twofold unit, as a dyad. Leo and Virgo also form such a bi-polar whole, which may account for the relationship between western Europe Christianity and Hebrew Palestine, for the Crusades and, before them, for the spread of Near East-

ern and Greek thought through Arab Spain. Thus the North
American continent as a whole integrates the head and throat
centers. But our present-day American society does not as
yet embody the most essential possibilities latent in the c o n-
t i n e n t of North America -- and we may have yet to see
what will develop in Canada, perhaps as a result of the shifting of the North Pole and of a basic change in climate.

PISCES ZONE: from 118°52' to 148°52'. The coastal region of California north of Santa Barbara, including the quite
magical coast of Big Sur and Carmel leading to the San Francisco Bay region, belongs to this zone. The sand dunes just
south of Pismo have a very psychic character; and, according to a now extinct theosophical group, The Temple of the
People, they were parts of ancient Lemuria, as was much of
the California coast further north. Mount Shasta, famous in
occult lore as the seat of an ancient Brotherhood, is found in
that Pisces zone (about 122° longitude) -- and so is Mount
Hood near Portland. British Columbia and the eastern part
of Alaska belongs to that zone also. Fairbanks, Alaska, is
here the cusp city (147°43'). Earthquakes in that region and
the next one (Aquarius zone) may indeed announce some important telluric upheavals. When I reached Southern California in 1920, the group with which I was associated had re-
ceived prophecies of the rise of parts of the old Lemurian
continent -- the e a s t e r n shores of which were supposed
to be the series of islands off the coast of Santa Barbara.
Such a rise would obviously produce huge tidal waves spreading over the lowlands of Southern California -- which may
account for what Edgar Cayce announced. The theory of the
slow, gradual shift of continents seems to me most logical
and acceptable.

AQUARIUS ZONE: from 148°52' to 178°52' west longitude.
The western part of Alaska, the Aleutian Islands and our new
State, Hawaii -- also the French Tahiti -- belong there. New

lands may well emerge in this zone.

CAPRICORN ZONE: from 178°52' west longitude to 151°08' east longitude. This zone includes, in the north, the eastern part of Siberia and, in the south, that of Australia. Sidney is located at 151°10'; Brisbane at 153°02'. New Zealand is also part of that zone of longitude, and a number of islands.

SAGITTARIUS ZONE: from 151°08' to 121°08' east longitude. This encompasses the islands of Japan, Korea and Manchuria and part of Siberia in the north. New Guinea and the larger part of Australia in the south. Also the Philippines above the equator. The conquering and expansive spirit of the Japanese people, in war or in business, may be attuned to this Sagittarian Earth-vibration; and this region of Siberia may have an ever-growing importance.

Thus we return to the Scorpio-Sagittarius cusp after having circumscribed the globe. In a certain sense, what we have done is to project the o r b i t of the Earth (ecliptic, or tropical zodiac) upon the g l o b e of the Earth. We have projected the c o s m i c reality of our planet (its orbit being its place and function in the entire solar system) upon its b i o-s p h e r i c reality. Our correlations had nothing to do with stars or constellations.

X. AS WE FACE THE FUTURE

Astrology is full of unsolved and perhaps insoluble problems, if it is considered to be anything but a symbolic language -- a kind of algebra -- enabling us to project patterns of order, derived from the cycles of motion of celestial bodies upon the confusing sequence of existential events on the Earth's biosphere, and especially in our human lives. It is for this reason that entirely different astrological systems can all work well in the hands of astrologers who are familiar with them and who apply them consistently and wisely. In some cases it can be assumed that they work at different levels; for instance, some astrologers have tried to prove that both the sidereal zodiac of constellations and the tropical zodiac of signs are valid, each referring to a certain aspect of life -- but there is very little agreement in defining these levels.

In discussing the two zodiacs in a previous chapter I stated that the problem concerning the zodiac of constellations was that no one could say why there was such a thing as a constellation -- some constellations grouping stars of different types, ages, and moving in different directions -- and, in any case, where the precise boundaries of these constellations were located. Even if we accept the claims of present-day advocates of a sidereal zodiac, claims based on what the Chaldean or Egyptian astrologers apparently used as a basis for their charts, this really need not warrant the confusion brought to modern astrological practice by the use of the archaic frame of reference. Why should we accept

Chaldean or Egyptian astrology any more than we accept the mythological stories of these long extinct cultures as foundations for our religious approach to the universe?

What I am saying here is that every great culture has its own set of symbols which express what is too deep and too vital to be formulated in rigidly intellectual and analytical or measurable terms. Even what we call modern science has its own basic postulates, its special type of logic, its own way of looking at existence; and this way has undergone a very profound transformation around the beginning of this century. There is no reason why we should not build a new kind of astrology; no reason why a new type of celestial frame of reference (a new zodiac) was not n e c e s s a r y after the great change in the deep mind of humanity during and after the sixth century B. C. which was also about the time when astrology began really to spread in the Hellenistic civilization via the Greek colonies in Asia Minor.

The tropical zodiac of signs also poses a basic problem which can probably be solved only in one of two ways; and neither of them is acceptable to everyone. That problem is the result of the fact that the seasons experienced in the moderate zones of the northern hemisphere are reversed in the southern hemisphere. When the Sun is in the sign, Aries, it is springtime in the northern hemisphere, but fall time south of the equator. For us, in the northern hemisphere, Aries is rightly a symbol of ebullient emergence into organic activity, of the impulsive and pioneering spirit. Can it be so also in the southern hemisphere when a person born with the Sun in Aries inhales at his first breath the autumnal air?

The advocates of the sidereal zodiac will say: didn't I tell you so? But their position raises also problems which are very important, especially at the psychological level. They still define the constellation Aries generally under terms suggesting birth at the beginning of spring, but the relationship between this constellation Aries and the beginning of spring is already invalid, and will become increasingly so. Thus the personal characteristics attributed to "birth with an Aries Sun" will have to be constantly altered, if the siderealist's approach is to be logical. This adds to the confusion. A person with the Sun around Aries 15° by sign, suddenly finds himself a "Piscean" according to the siderealist; yet his temperament may indeed be "typically Aries" according to the standard characterization. Hundreds of examples could be given. The point is: what is more important, the fact one is born in early spring (an incontrovertible fact), or the fact one is born with the Sun in a particular constellation created by the imagination of ancient people?

What is the solution of the problem in so far as an astrology based on the tropical-seasonal zodiac is concerned? The simpler solution is that Aries becomes Libra in the south hemisphere. Southern-hemispheric birth-charts should therefore have all their zodiacal signs reversed, so that if a person in Buenos Aires is born in early August his Sun is in Aquarius.

This solution has been strongly advocated by the now deceased French engineer-astrologer, D. Neroman, who founded in Paris the College Astrologique de France, wrote impressive, large volumes, and used a very remarkable gadget, the Domigraphe, to show clearly the state of the celestial sphere and the zodiac at every time for a number of latitudes. When I presented this solution in a magazine, one of the most vocal "siderealists" scornfully commented that this was absurd, because two men born at the same time less than a mile apart, but on either side of the exact equator, would have their natal Suns, one in Aries, the other in Libra. It is true that this seemingly does not make too much sense; but what this siderealist did not take into consideration is the possibility that actually the equatorial zone of the globe should have its own astrology -- and so should have, for other reasons, the polar zones. If the two hemispheres have each their own pole star, why should they not have, each, their own astrology? Why should there be only one astrology? This is the basic issue.

Stated this way, the problem takes on a greater and very significant scope, which, however, is partially modified by a second solution to the hemispheric difficulty just mentioned. This solution, stressed by Marc Edmund Jones, is that our present-day civilization is indeed "north hemispheric". It was born north of the Tropic of Cancer -- even in India -- and below the Arctic Circle.

What Marc Jones means, of course, is that our civilization brought its basic, not only conscious, but unconscious patterns of mind -- its fundamental symbols -- to the southern hemisphere. There may have been south-hemispheric centers of civilization in South America (the Incas) and in South Africa, but these no doubt had their own symbols, their own weltanschauung, and therefore their own astrology if they were actually born in this southern hemisphere. Any culture south of the equator which accepts our "north-hemispheric" astrology thereby reveals its essential dependence upon societies which built these mental concepts and ways of life in more or less temperate northern regions. This is true today of Australia, New Zealand, White South Africa, and even South America; they really are all as yet cultural colonies of European nations and almost totally dependent upon social, mental and artistic patterns of Europe.

A geographical observation tends to confirm this approach in terms of our geomorphic interpretation of the shapes of the continents. Not only can South America and Africa be considered to be downpointing triangular masses, but practically all peninsulas are also pointing downward from the northern regions -- witness Indo-China, India, Greece, Italy, Florida. In some cases, like Denmark and Normandy, which seem to be exceptions to the rule, we are probably dealing with regions which had been fairly recently parts of other lands just to the north.

Of course, this does not "prove" anything; but it suggests

that there are definite "lines of force" tending to flow southward from the north pole and to pull land masses in this southerly direction. This would mean that, indeed, our planet receives cosmic forces in the north polar regions, and that these forces are streaming southward, even below the equator. The point is here that this may be true at any time; so that, if a great original civilization should be found now located in the southern hemisphere, this would mean that when it was started, the poles were so placed that it actually was in the northern hemisphere of that time. In other words, it may very well be that all great civilizations originate in the northern hemisphere, that the southern hemisphere is like the negative polarity of the globe, that therefore astrology should be "north hemispheric". The location of the poles is not fixed; they were once at the place of what is now our equatorial belt and Antarctica and Northern Siberia were long ago warm lands. Thus it is always possible that the poles will shift again.

All this of course makes everything very confusing, unless one takes a strictly relativistic attitude and one does not consider whatever represent to us vitally significant symbols absolutely valid for the whole globe and for all times. This relativistic approach to knowledge, and to astrology among other manifestations of a particular civilization, is the one I have taken throughout my life. The zodiac of signs is our zodiac, now. It was probably not that of the Egyptian or Chaldean civilizations, and in India various systems are co-existing, very likely because Northern India and Southern India have basically two rather different cultures and two different groups of languages; but this need not be of any concern to us. Perhaps what concerns us today will not concern our descendants during the Aquarian Age, for then perhaps the whole concept of zodiac may appear meaningless.

I have shown recently in articles that astrology did not require the zodiac at all, any zodiac; that it could use in the near future a frame of reference provided by a twelvefold division of the s p a c e precisely surrounding the natal event, wherever it occurs (the true meaning of "Houses") -- or other frames of reference of a galactic character, once we become more conscious of the place of our solar system within the galaxy, and of its relation to other neighbors in this vast array of stars.

In a very real sense, astrology is derived from the symbolism of numbers. It is a kind of numerology; or, as I once said, of "arithmosophy" -- an applied wisdom of numbers. When astrologers link closely the twelve Houses of a chart with the twelve signs of the zodiac, or divide the projection of the ecliptic (the Earth's orbit) upon the galactic star-filled spaces into twelve constellations, all that they do is to refer the result of a twelvefold division of this ecliptic to the postulated symbolic meanings of the numbers one to twelve. We do the same thing when we divide the human body into twelve areas of organic functioning, or the Earth's globe into twelve longitude-zones, or any other type of zones. For some not too easily explainable reason man, in all times, has found some apparently universal meaning in numbers, series of numbers, numerical correlations, magic squares and in the results of many kinds of numerical operations. God geometrizes -- the Greeks said. The Hebrew Kabbalah, and similar Indian and Chinese systems, are based on numbers. India apparently discovered the mysterious no-number, 0 -- and this probably correlated with the development of a new and transcendent approach to existence and to the universe.

Thus many systems; yet a quite fundamental sequence of meanings connected with defined sequences of numbers related to the structural unfoldment of a variety of existential processes.

Number, to the modern mind, refers to the frequency of vibrations; and we explain the whole universe now in terms of vibrations and waves. Any process implies a numerable sequence of structured phases. No one should mistake the first for the second or the fourth or the seventh phase; this, whatever be the type of material substance or mental concept the process deals with. The important point, however, is that we should define well the process as a whole and its space-time field of operation, when we are studying the sequence of its phases. The danger lies in the fact that we tend to see the particular process we are analyzing as being THE life-process.

This is the great trouble with all types of human knowledge and in particular with astrological systems. Every culture has considered itself the center of the world of Man. Every people has, subtly or crudely, felt, at least at one time of its development, to be the Elect People, the Vanguard of Civilization; and our Western civilization has indeed not failed to speak of "Civilization", as if there were no other civilization -- at least until the important and revealing work of Arnold Toynbee. Most men believe there is only one Civilization that counts, one Science, one Astrology: their own. They see the earth-structure absolutely anchored at the Greenwich meridian, and claim, with intense conviction, that "civilization moves westward". Nevertheless there may very well have been at some more or less distant time an "eastward" movement that sent the remnants of the fabled, yet most probably very real, Atlantean civilization across Europe, Africa and the Mediterranean Sea to Egypt, the Near East, and perhaps to South India. Should we really speak of only one wave of civilization?

THE MARCH OF CIVILIZATION

A number of astrologers have done so, believing that one could trace the westward progress of great centers of civilization in terms of the precessional rhythm of one degree every 72 years. If one considers it feasible to project the constellations of the zodiac upon the Earth-globe in a permanent, "fixed" manner, then the signs of the zodiac can be said to progress westward; that is to say, the vernal equinox point is seen to move one degree every 72 years on the surface of the globe, completing the round-the-world trip not in "80 days" but in less than 26,000 years.

This long round-the-globe advance would be what I once called, in a series of articles in the American Astrology magazine (1946-47) "The March of Civilization". I was careful, however, to point out (1) that we should not think that great historical events, as factors in the rise of civilization, occurred o n l y at the assumed passage of the moving equinox point (the "crest" of the wave of civilization) over a particular zone of longitude, and (2) that, if the location of this moving wave-crest at a particular time did n o t correspond to a most significant high-point in the evolution of the mind and in the cultural achievements of the people living in that location, then the whole scheme was meaningless, or the given point of departure was obviously wrong.

The point of departure used by the Pyramid-oriented group of astrologers was and is still the correspondence between the mid-point of the so-called Taurean Age (Taurus 15°) and the longitude of the Great Pyramid (32°08' east longitude). This means that the crest of the wave of civilization would have been passing through the longitude of the Pyramid around 3500 B.C. Egyptologists apparently believe that the Pharoah Menes whose reign supposedly began the First Dynasty of the Old Kingdom lived near that time; Memphis is said to have been founded then. If this were the case, however, the wave-crest would have been forty-five degrees west of the Pyramid's longitude in about 360 B.C. (i. e. 45 times 72 years later), thus at nearly 13° west longitude -- which means in the Atlantic Ocean, or leaving the west coast of North Africa. Does it sound logical to make the crest of the wave of civilization leave the westmost land in Europe and enter the ocean when tremendously significant developments were occurring in Greece, and as well in Persia, India and China?

According to Edward Johndro, Aries 0° is supposed to have corresponded geographically to the meridian of west longitude 29° plus, some thirty years ago, Paul Council said it corresponded to about west longitude 36°. He wrote that the crest of the wave was reaching the extreme eastern tip of Brazil, adding: "Can it be doubted that this point is the mean geographic and spiritual focus of civilization and world-evolution today?" ("Cosmic Causation in Geophysics", page 5). This hardly seems to be a very logical statement, considering where the main centers of civilization are today.

What I attempted to show in the series of articles written about twenty years ago was simply that there seems to be indeed a westward march of civilization and that the precessional measure of "one degree equals seventy-two years" can be used quite significantly to map out the progress of this westward march.* What I then suggested was that, on historical grounds, we could significantly assume that the crest of this wave of civilization was passing through the longitude of Greece in the middle of the sixth century B.C. I took 550 B.C. as a convenient starting point.

From 550 B.C. to 200 B.C. the Greek culture marked the apex of human progress in the Western world. Then the emphasis began to shift toward Italy. The Rome meridian was reached around 303 A.D., just before the reign of Constantine the Great who made of Christianity the imperial religion. As the Roman empire disintegrated, the spotlight kept moving westward and northward, and when Charlemagne's rule began the cycle of our Christian-European culture, the wave-crest had reached the Rhine, and the capital of Charlemagne's empire Aachen (6° east longitude). It reached the meridian of Paris about the time of the first Crusade (eleventh century), whose leaders were mostly no-

---

*A westward motion is also found on a much smaller scale in the growth of cities, at least in our historical period. Cities, and especially their residential sections for the "elite", tend to develop westward, unless blocked by natural obstacles.

blemen from the Paris and Normandy region. This was the great age of Medieval France.

The wave-crest came to the Greenwich meridian around 1177 A.D., near the time of the beginnings of the Oxford University and the Magna Charta (1215), foundation for the English brand of democracy. As England grew in power, the wave-crest moved westward, crossed Ireland after 1600 A.D. and it left the westernmost coast of Ireland ($10\frac{1}{2}^{0}$ longitude) in 1933, the very year Hitler came to power in Germany, and F.D. Roosevelt in America -- and suddenly the spotlight of history seemed to turn to the East coast of the United States.

If we go back from the sixth century B.C. we see that the westward moving vernal equinox point (the crest of the wave) reached the shores of Egypt on the Red Sea at about the time of the great religious reformer Akhnaton (eastern longitude $35\frac{1}{2}^{0}$); as this Pharaoh might be called the father of Western monotheism, this correlation may mark the beginning of this part of the Egyptian past which belongs truly to our Western civilization. Before that time, the wave-crest moved through Mesopotamia (longitude 44^{0}-45^{0}) at the time of Hammurabi in Babylon; and it was located at the Indus Valley around 3800-4000 B.C. which was presumably the period during which an important culture developed, whose ruins were discovered not so long ago. Earlier than this no dates are really reliable.

WAVE OR WAVES?

This brief sketch of the growth of civilization during our historical times obviously leaves many questions unanswered. Why should we think that this westward progress refers to CIVILIZATION? It may well have meaning only in terms of our Western civilization and its roots in the past. While Greece was at its cultural apex, India's culture at Gautama Buddha's time not only flourished -- as Greek travellers at the time of Alexander's short-lived conquest related -- but with the Buddha a movement of the greatest significance be-

gan in India which spread eastward to Indo China and northward to China and Japan. China has its great civilization,
and so had the Incas and the Mayan-Aztecs regions. Nor did
I mention the swift spread of Islam in all directions at a time
when the crest-wave would have been passing through Switzerland and Provence. Obviously the picture of a single wave
of civilization is one-sided and inadequate.

Nevertheless it seems evident that there are waves of
civilization -- or shall we say waves of dynamic intensity
within the formative Mind of our Earth; and perhaps also ed-
dies or whirlpools of civilization. The rotation of our globe
produces certain definite effects upon the atmosphere; it gives
rise to trade-winds and monsoons quite regular in their annual patterns, but also to tornadoes and hurricanes, which
interestingly enough revolve clockwise or counter-clockwise
depending upon the hemisphere in which they occur. Why not
accept also as a related fact that human collectivities and
their ability to give cultural forms to their sense of value and
to build institutions are affected, like the atmosphere, by
forces emanating from the Earth-as-a-whole, and as well
from the state of the solar system and the entire galaxy. As
we do not know as yet what these forces are, our religions
have transcendentalized and personalized them as gods or
archangels, devas or nature-spirits. We have also created
around them a mythological astrology with its zodiacal pictures and its mysterious "influences".

My aim, in this and other books, is to reintegrate Man
within the organic whole -- the global field of organized and
interdependent activities -- of the planet Earth. The symbol
of the globe is the most fundamental one of the expected "New
Age". Applied to the human person it leads us to the concept
of what I have called "the man of plenitude" -- the total, ful-
filled, productive individual person. What the conceptual
images of geodetic equivalents and of a wave or waves of civilization should essentially convey to us is that this Earth is
"alive", that it vibrates and pulsates, from the ionosphere

to its unknown core -- which may very well be a peculiar kind of "void" from which unknown forces operate.

Returning again to the postulated wave of civilization: this wave has not only a crest, or crests, but also a trough. What we call the vernal equinox is only one point in the yearly process of relationship between the Earth and the Sun. There are two equinoxes, and two solstices. When I wrote the series of articles "The March of Civilization" in 1946 I could say with great timeliness: "The wave of civilization covers the whole globe. It has a trough as well as a wave. And the trough is located in the longitude of the Marshall Islands, near Bikini Atoll! A "coincidence" perhaps, but a significant one. This trough was located at about 170° west longitude because the crest (according to my pattern of wave-unfoldment) was at about $10\frac{1}{2}$ east longitude. The trough of the wave corresponds to the fall equinox (Libra 0°); and Neptune was practically on that degree of the tropical celestial zodiac when the Chicago experiments were conducted which led in December 1942 to the first man-made atomic chain reation.

The "solstice point" in this wave of civilization then referred to the longitude of Mexico City, Texas, South Dakota and Lake Winnipeg (Canada) -- and on the other hand to the longitude of Colombo (Ceylon), Madras (India) and the Tibetan-Kashmir border and the Chinese-Siberian borders -- the last two regions becoming soon after important fields of international tension. But this is not all, for in-between the equinoxes and the solstices stand the mid-points of the fixed signs of the zodiac, sometimes referred to as "Avataric Gates", i.e. as points of release of great energy, constructive or destructive as the case may be. Thus a point 45-degrees behind the crest of the wave, or ahead of it, could be significant centers of events related to the whole global pattern -- the ever-flowing pattern -- of civilization. As the crest is (according to my calculations) nearing 11° west longitude, we find 45 degrees back (i.e. to the east) a zone of

stress and strain at 34° east longitude; and this is the longi-
tude of Palestine (Jerusalem 35°, Tel Aviv 34°, the Gulf of
Acaba 35°) -- also of part of Rhodesia to the south, and of
Soviet Russia to the north.

Forty-five degrees to the west of the wave-crest we find
in South America a much disturbed Guiana, and the Buenos
Aires-Montevideo region. One hundred and thirty-five degrees west of the wave-crest we find the longitude of our recent State, Alaska -- Fairbanks is located at $147\frac{1}{2}°$.

This of course does not explain the importance of the United States in the present-day world; and this raises the question of whether a new "wave of civilization" did not begin at
the time of the Declaration of Independence -- or whether
what is developing this century in our country, original a
departure as it may seem, should not rather be considered
as an extension of European civilization -- greatly magnified
and nearly monstrous in its physical-intellectual as well as
political-industrial development, but nevertheless not a truly
independent starting point. The c o n t i n e n t of North America may very well be, after probable telluric transformations, the "cradle for a New Race", as modern Theosophists
have been claiming for nearly a century; but we may witness
today only the earliest prenatal stage of the
formation of that New Race.

Western civilization is still overshadowing the whole planet -- directly or in terms of the violent reaction against its
premises which it is eliciting. Soviet Russia is, of course,
part of that Western civilization, just as Byzanteum and Rome
were two parts of the Mediterranean Greco-Latin civilization. And, in terms of our present location of wave-crest
which we have been discussing, Western civilization is a t
s e a! It has been so, we found, since about 1933 and the
Nazi purgation of the Western world. But "being at sea" may
be a very significant situation; for it may mean that we have
returned to the great Womb of the biosphere, t h e o n e
O c e a n. And indeed if anything is basic in this tormented

period of ours it is the tremendous importance of the "Collective Unconscious"--which could mean, fairly soon, a return to chaos. In fact we may be passing, on a planetary time-scale, through the very moment of planetary Fecundation preceding the prenatal beginning of a truly new Age, this moment lasting three centuries -- what I have called the Avataric Cycle.

AN OCEANIC AGE

The Aquarian Age may be, far more than we think now, an o c e a n i c Age. The Great Voyages of the fifteenth century (500 years before the start of the Aquarian Age, according to my hypothesis) were only the very beginning of the story. The Piscean Age began when Rome came to claim the Mediterranean as m a r e   n o s t r u m (our sea). England in her way repeated the boast last century: P a x   B r i t a n n i c a paralleled P a x   R o m a n a. We, in America, have been trying to continue England's role after her global collapse as ruler of the seas; but this role is a trap now. We are challenged at every step by Soviet Russia; indeed we are like "Enemy Twins" scowling at each other but fated to work together, in spite of our puerile disagreements and siblings' jealousy, as we face an aroused Third World -- the new "Barbarians", not only at our gates, but inside of our gates.

All our constructions may thus, symbolically if not literally, topple down into the One Ocean; for now we should have realized, and we will have to realize, that our giving different names to various seas and gulfs is symbolically meaningless, for there is but o n e ocean, one planetary-biospheric Womb. And we must return to it, in mind if not in our distraught and deluged physical bodies. Perhaps the new focusing of man's attention upon oceanography and the possible use of the ocean's floor for food-production and mining as well as for warfare shows the direction in which mankind is moving. Of course we are also reaching to the Moon, and eventually other planets of the solar system, but in a

sense the atmosphere, stratosphere and all that ancient astrologers called the sub-lunar sphere form also a kind of ocean in which the Earth-globe as a whole is bathing.

It is quite possible that the entire new Age, which I see
rather as Phase Two of the vast Great Sidereal Year than as
the "Aquarian Age", will be essentially a period during which
mankind will be concerned above all with the realization of
its oceanic spiritual depth of planetary being, of its fundamental common humanity. I believe that mental pictures of
a New Age being spread around, either by college professors
of the Rand organization type (the "prospectivists" employed
by the government and by big business to evaluate future
prospects) or, at the other end of the mind-spectrum, by devotees of "New Age ideals", are likely not to correspond
closely to the realities of life some two centuries ahead. I
would rather trust the last-mentioned group -- over-idealistic as its visions may be -- for it at least seems to realize
that our present-day type of technology is not the answer,
and that the one basic factor in the future will be a transformation of human nature and the appearance perhaps of new
faculities. What we call now telepathy is only a beginning.

Humanity, at least Western world humanity, may indeed
be entering the "sea" of a far more fluid, vast and mobile
consciousness. And this quite likely will involve a profound
change in the social organization of mankind, perhaps in the
quantity of human beings on the globe, and in its distribution
upon the continents. Continents may be breaking down into
smaller units. There could be unity in oceanic, sub-and-
supra-conscious depths of being; yet at the same time a greater scatteredness of human collectivities in close contact with
the sea, yet as well in close, immediate and vital communication with each other through new forms of transportation
and through a "trans-physical", mental and super-mental
sharing of variegated experiences. This is, at least as I envision the future in a few centuries. But before this state is
reached, the going is likely to be very rough -- the oceanic

state has undoubtedly many violent storms in store for mankind.

As we reach this "oceanic" stage of geo-social development of mankind it is entirely possible that what I have presented as a wave of civilization will also be dissolved into the gradually calmed sea. We may reach a truly global condition of all-human planet-wide (and planetary) development in which there will be more than ever a multiplicity of foci of human evolution on quite a few "islands" of culture, geographically separated, but sooner or later spiritually integrated into a global whole, Man.

If however, the wave-concept is still applicable, and my estimate of the present location of the wave-crest is correct, then we can expect Brazil to become the main, or most dynamic, focus of a more reintegrated and more closely stabilized humanity during Phase Three of the Great Sidereal Year, the so-called "Capricorn Age" which should begin in about twenty-two centuries. A few occultists have claimed recently that there was, three or four decades ago, a transfer of great beings wielding planetary power from Tibet to the Peruvian Andes -- this evidently because of what they knew was going to happen in Tibet and in China. This may be occult fiction, or fact; I can produce no personal verification either way, but I tend to accept the story as referring to facts.

Whatever form North and Central America will have at the end of the so-called "Capricorn" Age may well be then the location for the great "American" civilization and a truly new race of human beings. It will be Phase Four of the Great Year, and this "Sagittarian" Age should be an Age of concretization of spiritual values. I repeat that I tend to believe that some of the expectations people have today for the coming Aquarian Age (Phase Two) will only mature into actualities during this Phase Four. This will occur some five thousand years after the end of the 19th century, and ten thousand years after what old India believed to be the start of Kali

Yuga in 3102 B. C.

Human beings today are extraordinarly in a hurry. We are witnessing a prodigious acceleration of the rhythm of human and mental evolution; and our modern intellectuals in their fondness for extrapolating present trends into the future announce even more fantastic developments ahead -- indeed very near. According to the calculations of some French scientists who founded the new "science", la prospective, a climactic point is to be reached next century -- indeed, perhaps significantly, very near the date I have arrived at for the beginning of the Aquarian Age. There may be a kernel of truth in such predictions, but as I stated in earlier chapters, the last twelve years of this century may upset greatly such "scientific" predictions.

The most important thing is not that one should build precise theories and rigorous systems, valuable as these may be to give us a sense of structural destiny and purpose in the midst of bewildering and seemingly chaotic events. It is to face the future with courage, faith and a quality of "vision" -- with a deep and unchallengeable intuition of individual destiny, inner stability and peace. We may be able to acquire these through subjective meditation and identification with superiod, or "eonic" Minds; but this may be a difficult path for many individuals and it is for them that studies such as this, which attempt to help individuals (and mankind as a whole) to find their place and function in time and space, can be of great value if approached with an open mind unobstructed by past traditions and semantic blockages.

EPILOGUE

EPILOGUE

In this volume I have sought to extend and deepen the consciousness of the reader by integrating the present moment and his or her experience of change and radical crisis in vast historical as well as astrological cycles, and by relating local problems to the broad spaces of an Earth considered as an organized system of interdependent activities, and indeed of organic functions. But it is obvious that everything for an individual human being begins with his or her individual person.

If it is necessary today to overcome the naive idea that society is made up of individuals, considered abstractly as free, equal, independent entities essentially external to their environment and the patterns of thoughts, feelings, behavior and language which conditioned, and largely determined their personalities, nevertheless it would be senseless to go to the other extreme and to make of individual persons only the products of social, economic or telluric conditions. What I have been saying is that the development of a human being into an individual person is conditioned by the frames of reference which he consciously or unconsciously accepts -- and accept he must, whether he admits the fact or not, for every single event or inner change can only acquire meaning and some sort of however imprecise purpose or value when related to an over-all frame of reference. Every man has a philosophy and a cosmology; he follows at any time a certain way of life and thinks in terms of particular language. If he is not aware he is doing so, and he has never consciously or deliberately thought about philosophical ideas or the nature of the universe, this simply means that he takes for granted the traditional approach and the frames of reference of his family, class, nation and civilization.

As I stated repeatedly, by far the larger portion of mankind has so far used only or at least predominantly l o c a l frames of reference. Even its gods, as far as the bulk of mankind was concerned, have been until fairly recently (historically speaking) local gods. The concept of a universal God, after it developed in the human mind, was strongly colored with localism, or else it was so abstract and transcendent as to deny any significant reality and value to the world we live in. Indeed it operated in so many cases as a negative frame of reference; for the God-Idea, when personalized, embodied all that man felt unable to attain, even if he wanted so much to do so; for instance, omnipotence, omnipresence, perfect love, supreme untarnishable beauty, etc.

A frame of reference a g a i n s t which you give meaning -- a more or less negative meaning -- to the facts of your existence is not a wholesome one. Thus mysticism developed on the basis of the striving for complete identification with God. If there is such an identification, any frame of reference loses any real meaning; but also existence as a separate individual loses its ultimate value.

True, there is much beauty and significance in the mystic's aspiration to the "unitive state", just as there is great meaning to moments of pause and inward withdrawal in the midst of tense outer activity. But this aspiration constitutes only one side of the human situation. Unity implies multiplicity. The transcendence of God implies the condition of cosmic existence; and as Zen masters keep repeating to their aware disciples n i r v a n a and s a m s a r a are one. It is as an expression of the everlasting relationship between nirvana and samsara, between One and the Many that frames of reference operate. They exist inevitably for all forms of consciousness. The only issue is how inclusive, how steady and shock-proof -- yet adjustable and extendable -- is your frame of reference as an individual person.

My belief is that today the one truly operational frame of reference for man is the planet, Earth, considered as a cosmic type of "organism" within which humanity as a whole fulfills a basic function -- a function which, for lack of a more accurate analogy, we can compare to that of the cerebro-spinal nervous system in the human body. It is Man's function in the economy of the earth to transmute into consciousness the results of all that he collectively experiences as he comes in contact with all regions of the globe. And as really to understand anything objectively one must gain a more or less distant perspective on it, the recent acquired ability of mankind to place itself, directly or by T. V. proxy, outside of the globe has indeed great value, even if this was made possible by an essentially destructive (matter-destroying and Earth-poisoning) type of technology.

Man needs a frame of reference in order to situate, evaluate and give a coherent and consistent meaning to his experiences; but, alas, most men not only accept unconsciously and never question the frame of reference embodied in their culture, religion and their social-political-economic patterns of existence, but they have a remarkable way of straight-jacketing their minds and activities in terms of the profession they adopt or the type of study or technique they eagerly, and perhaps fanatically, pursue. And this, to me, is the saddest part of the human picture today; it has not even the value of the allegiance of men of the past to a caste or a guild, rooted as these were in a quite profound awareness of essential human and collective needs.

I am speaking here, for instance, of the type of attitude which expresses itself in the phrase "art for art's sake", or science for science's sake, knowledge for knowledge's sake regardless of consequences to humanity. Power (social or political) for power's sake, success for success's sake (the

"American success story"), could be added to the list -- and in the field to which this book is related, a s t r o l o g y   f o r   a s t r o l o g y ' s   s a k e. An eminent personality in the field of American astrology has recently been quoted as saying: It is not what astrology does for you which counts, but what you do for astrology. This is the "professional" attitude in its most extreme form.

To me, astrology has no meaning or value except it helps man to understand better his innate potentialities, the unfoldment of these potentialities, and the development of humanity through the centuries and with reference to the planet's biosphere within which it should operate as a harmonious force for further evolutionary growth. Indeed, as I see it, there is no such thing as astrology p e r   s e, as an independent entity having strictly defined methods of operation absolutely valid under any circumstances. As I stated already I consider astrology as a symbolical language. Every language has evidently its own syntax and vocabulary, and a "genius" of its own, but here again making of the language an entity for the sake of which -- of its so-called purity or perfection -- the mind of an individual person has to become patterned in its expression by a rigid formalism is, as I see it, an unwholesome procedure. At least it is so t o d a y, in a period of total reorientation of consciousness and revaluation of our symbols and institutions.·

We should accept the most radically transforming implications of this period of human evolution; and I am speaking of "evolution" instead of "history" because it is not only the future of our present civilization which is at stake but the future of the whole biosphere, of the whole Earth. And this is why I believe that the puny efforts of contemporary man at destroying himself and earthly life, on the pretense of glorifying himself as master of all natural processes, biological as well as atomic, wil be frustrated. In which way our human pride will be frustrated, I do not claim to know; but because of this belief I feel that the individuals who have understood this tragic potentiality inherent in the coming decades should come together and, in as little obvious a way as possible, should establish "seed groups" from which in due time a new kind of humanity may arise.

At the end of the cycle of the year all that belongs to the realm of the leaves of the yearly plants inevitably decays; but the seeds remain, as hidden centers from which the new life will spring. What humanity needs now are seed-men and women willing and ready to assume the sacred task of self-metamorphosis, individually yet in constant relationship to one another -- self-metamorphosis not merely for their own spiritual growth but for the sake of humanity. I have stressed this need for "seed-men" for the last fifty years, and all my work has been oriented toward the goal of making the few people I could reach clearly aware and deeply concerned with what this need for seed-men implies.

One cannot reach a state of mental clarity and of "ultimate concern" (as theologians now say) if one does not experience a deep surge of unchallengeable faith, courage and persistence, even under the most difficult circumstances. Both the mind and the deepest emotions must be set aflame by what one has come to realize is true and undismissable evidence. This is not a matter of analysis, research or scholarship, but one of total involvement and total response. And as conclusion to the effort represented by this book, may I therefore hope that whoever reads it will find out of this experience greater faith, greater courage, a wider vision and a more inclusive love for mankind and for the Earth -- so that he or she may indeed become a vibrant, dynamic, unafraid seed-foundation for the impending rebirth of civilization on a purified "Aquarian" Earth-globe!

INDEX

INDEX